Ethernet Configuration Guidelines

A Quick Reference Guide to the Official Ethernet (IEEE 802.3) Configuration Rules

Charles Spurgeon

Peer-to-Peer Communications, Inc.

The diagram on the cover was drawn by Dr. Robert M. Metcalfe in 1976 to present Ethernet for the first time. It was used in his presentation to the National Computer Conference in June of that year. On the drawing are the original terms for describing Ethernet. Since then other terms have come into usage among Ethernet enthusiasts.
From <u>The Ethernet Sourcebook</u>, ed. Robyn E. Shotwell (New York: North-Holland, 1985), title page.

Cover diagram reproduced with permission.

Published by Peer-to-Peer Communications, Inc.
P.O. Box 640218
San Jose
California 95164-0218
Phone: 800-420-2677
Fax: 408-435-0895

For a catalog of Peer-to-Peer Communications' other titles, please contact the publisher.

Cover: Althea Perley, New York, NY
Printing: George Lithograph, Brisbane, CA

ISBN 1-57398-012-9
Printed in the United States of America

10 9 8 7 6 5 4 3 2 1

Many of the designations used by manufacturers and sellers to distinguish their products are claimed as trademarks. Where those designations appear in this book, and the author was aware of a trademark claim, the designations have been printed in initial capital letters or all capital letters.

Portions of the information contained herein are Copyright © 1993,1994,1995 by the Institute of Electrical and Electronics Engineers, Inc. The IEEE disclaims any responsibility or liability resulting from the placement and use in this publication. Information is reprinted with the permission of the IEEE.

NOTICE: The examples and other information in this book are intended solely as teaching aids and should not be applied to any particular network without independent verification. Independent verification is especially important in any application in which an incorrect network design could result in loss of data or time.

For these reasons, while every effort was made to provide accurate information, there is no warranty expressed or implied that the examples, specifications, or other information shown here are free of error, or that they will meet the requirements of any particular network application.

Table of Contents

Table of Contents

Table of Contents

Preface

Once upon a time, back in the early Packetozoic,[1] Ethernet was simple and easy to configure. There was only one media system, based on a heavy-duty "thick" coaxial cable, and the configuration rules for that system could be listed in a couple of sentences. As Ethernet caught on and became steadily more popular, clever engineers extended the capabilities of Ethernet again and again. They invented thin coaxial Ethernet, and twisted-pair Ethernet, and fiber optic Ethernet. Not content with that, they invented the 100 megabit per second variety of Ethernet.

This wide range of media systems provides enormous flexibility and make it possible to design an Ethernet LAN to fit virtually every circumstance. However, all this flexibility does have a price: the varieties of Ethernet media each have their own bits and pieces of equipment and their own configuration rules, which makes the system a lot more complex than things were in the old days. This book helps deal with the complexity by listing the official configuration rules in a set of self-contained chapters that are designed as quick reference guides to the territory.

---

1. An era that lasted roughly from the origins of experimental Ethernet until the invention of new media varieties in the 1980s.

The rules in this book can all be found in the Ethernet standards for each media system. However, the formal standards are not usually stocked in bookstores. To help make things simpler, this book collects the configuration rules in one place, which means that you don't have to pay high prices to buy the standards documents and then wade through the formal standards language trying to extract all of the rules yourself.

The intent of this book is to answer typical questions about Ethernet configuration, including the maximum segment length for a given media type, and the rules for linking segments together. This is not a general guide on how to use Ethernet equipment or how to design networks, nor does it explain how to build cables and media systems. While there is a small amount of tutorial information included, most of what you will find here is page after page of Ethernet configuration rules, including all those three-letter acronyms[2] that the computer industry seems to thrive on.

What This Book Includes

This book describes the configuration rules for seven media varieties from the official IEEE Ethernet standard. For the original 10-Mbps system, this includes the following media varieties:

- 10BASE5 thick coax
- 10BASE2 thin coax
- 10BASE-T twisted-pair
- 10BASE-FL fiber optic

For the 100-Mbps Fast Ethernet system, this includes the following varieties:

- 100BASE-TX twisted-pair
- 100BASE-T4 twisted-pair
- 100BASE-FX fiber optic

---

2. Called TLAs, of course.

A few standard and non-standard media varieties have been developed over the years that have not seen wide usage. They are not covered in this book. The varieties from the IEEE standard that are not covered include the broadband cable variety (10BROAD36), which was designed for use over cable TV systems, and the 1-Mbps twisted-pair variety (1BASE5), which is a slower twisted-pair system that never became widely used.

There have also been a number of vendor-specific innovations developed over the years that are not part of the official standard and that operate at various speeds. Examples of vendor-specific systems include 5-Mbps broadband cable segments as well as several wireless channels. These vendor-specific systems are not covered in this guide because they are not part of the formal specifications, and are therefore not described in the official configuration guidelines.

How to Use This Book

If you know which variety of media segment you're interested in, you can jump right to the chapter that describes the configuration rules for it. Also, Appendix A provides a summary of the 10-Mbps segment rules, and Appendix B provides a summary of the 100-Mbps segment rules.

This book begins with a brief Ethernet tutorial which describes the basic operation of the Ethernet system, and those features of the system that are common to all media varieties. Following the tutorial are two sets of chapters, one covering the 10-Mbps and the other covering the 100-Mbps media varieties.

The chapters on the 10-Mbps media segments begin with a chapter which introduces the 10-Mbps media system, describing the features that are common to all 10-Mbps media segments. Similarly, the chapters on 100-Mbps Fast Ethernet segments begin with a chapter which introduces the 100-Mbps media system, and that describes the features common to all 100-Mbps media segments.

The chapters on individual media segments follow these introductory chapters. Each variety of 10-Mbps and 100-Mbps Ethernet media segment is briefly described in a separate chapter, including the configuration guidelines for a single segment of the media type being described.

At the end of the individual media segment chapters are chapters on the multi-segment configuration guidelines for the 10-Mbps and 100-Mbps systems. These chapters describe how multiple segments that operate at a given speed may be combined to form larger Ethernet systems. The media segment chapters and the multi-segment configuration chapters are designed as self-contained references. For that reason, some small portions of text are repeated in these chapters.

If you want to link Ethernet segments that operate at different speeds you must use a bridge or switching hub, therefore Chapter 15 briefly describes how bridges and switching hubs work.

Acknowledgments

I would like to thank Bob Metcalfe and his fellow researchers at Xerox PARC for inventing Ethernet in the first place. The acumen that underlies the original design for Ethernet is reflected in its remarkable success. I would also like to thank the scores of engineers who have voluntarily given their time in countless IEEE standards meetings over the years to help extend the Ethernet system and to write the specifications.

I also thank William C. Bard, manager of the Networking Services group at the Computation Center of the University of Texas at Austin, for supporting my writing efforts. I especially thank William Green and Rich Seifert for critically reading the manuscript and for providing a number of useful suggestions.

Most importantly, I would like to thank my wife, Joann Zimmerman, for enduring yet another book project, and for her patience, her support, and her editing skills. Without her, this book would not have been possible.

CHAPTER 1   A Brief Tutorial on the Ethernet System

1.1 The Ethernet System

This chapter provides a brief tutorial on the Ethernet system. We'll begin with the origins of Ethernet and the Ethernet standards, and then describe the essential features of Ethernet operation.

Ethernet is a local area network (LAN)[1] technology that transmits information between computers at speeds of 10 and 100 million bits per second (Mbps). Currently the most widely used version of Ethernet technology is the 10-Mbps twisted-pair variety.

The 10-Mbps Ethernet media varieties include the original thick coaxial system, as well as thin coaxial, twisted-pair, and fiber optic systems. The most recent Ethernet standard defines the new 100-Mbps Fast Ethernet system which operates over twisted-pair and fiber optic media.

1.2 Ethernet is a Popular, Vendor-Neutral Network Technology

There are several LAN technologies in use today, but Ethernet is by far the most popular. Industry estimates indicate that as of 1994 over

---

1. A LAN is defined as a privately owned data communications system that usually covers a limited territory, hence the term "local area."

40 million Ethernet nodes had been installed worldwide. The widespread popularity of Ethernet ensures that there is a large market for Ethernet equipment, which also helps keep the technology competitively priced.

From the time of the first Ethernet standard, the specifications and the rights to build Ethernet technology have been made easily available to anyone. This openness, combined with the ease of use and robustness of the Ethernet system, resulted in a large Ethernet market and is another reason Ethernet is so widely implemented in the computer industry.

The vast majority of computer vendors today equip their products with 10-Mbps Ethernet attachments, making it possible to link all manner of computers with an Ethernet LAN. As the 100-Mbps standard becomes more widely adopted, computers are being equipped with an Ethernet interface[2] that operates at both 10-Mbps and 100-Mbps. The ability to link a wide range of computers using a vendor-neutral network technology is an essential feature for today's LAN managers. Most LANs must support a wide variety of computers purchased from different vendors, which requires a high degree of network interoperability of the sort that Ethernet provides.

1.3 Development of Ethernet Standards

Ethernet was invented at the Xerox Palo Alto Research Center in the 1970s by Dr. Robert M. Metcalfe. It was designed to support research on the "office of the future," which included one of the world's first personal workstations, the Xerox Alto. The first Ethernet system ran at approximately 3-Mbps and was known as "experimental Ethernet."

---

2. An Ethernet interface is also referred to as an "adapter," "controller", "interface card," and "network interface card (NIC)." All of these terms refer to the same thing: the set of electronics in a computer that provide a connection to an Ethernet.

Formal specifications for Ethernet were published in 1980 by a multi-vendor consortium that created the DEC-Intel-Xerox (DIX) standard. This effort turned the experimental Ethernet into an open, production-quality Ethernet system that operates at 10-Mbps. Ethernet technology was then adopted for standardization by the LAN standards committee of the Institute of Electrical and Electronics Engineers (IEEE 802).

The IEEE standard was first published in 1985, with the formal title of "IEEE 802.3 Carrier Sense Multiple Access with Collision Detection (CSMA/CD) Access Method and Physical Layer Specifications." The IEEE standard has since been adopted by the International Organization for Standardization (ISO), which makes it a worldwide networking standard.

The IEEE standard provides an "Ethernet like" system based on the original DIX Ethernet technology. All Ethernet equipment since 1985 is built according to the IEEE 802.3 standard, which is pronounced "eight oh two dot three." To be absolutely accurate, then, we should refer to Ethernet equipment as "IEEE 802.3 CSMA/CD" technology. However, most of the world still knows it by the original name of Ethernet, and that's what we'll call it as well.

The 802.3 standard is periodically updated to include new technology. Since 1985 the standard has grown to include new media systems for 10-Mbps Ethernet (e.g. twisted-pair media), as well as the latest set of specifications for 100-Mbps Fast Ethernet.

1.4 Elements of the Ethernet System

The Ethernet system consists of three basic elements: 1. the physical medium used to carry Ethernet signals between computers, 2. a set of medium access control rules embedded in each Ethernet interface that allow multiple computers to fairly arbitrate access to the shared Ethernet channel, and 3. an Ethernet frame that consists of a standardized set of bits used to carry data over the system.

The following chapters describe the configuration rules for the first element, the physical media segments. Next we'll take a quick look at the second and third elements; the set of medium access control rules in Ethernet, and the Ethernet frame.

1.5 Operation of Ethernet

Each Ethernet-equipped computer, also known as a station, operates independently of all other stations on the network: there is no central controller. All stations attached to an Ethernet are connected to a shared signaling system, also called the medium. Ethernet signals are transmitted serially, one bit at a time, over the shared signal channel to every attached station. To send data a station first listens to the channel, and when the channel is idle the station transmits its data in the form of an Ethernet frame, or packet.[3]

After each frame transmission, all stations on the network must contend equally for the next frame transmission opportunity. This ensures that access to the network channel is fair, and that no single station can lock out the other stations. Access to the shared channel is determined by the medium access control (MAC) mechanism embedded in the Ethernet interface located in each station. The medium access control mechanism is based on a system called Carrier Sense Multiple Access with Collision Detection (CSMA/CD).

The CSMA/CD Protocol

The CSMA/CD protocol functions somewhat like a dinner party in a dark room. Everyone around the table must listen for a period of quiet before speaking (Carrier Sense). Once a space occurs everyone has an equal chance to say something (Multiple Access). If two people start talking at the same instant they detect that fact, and quit speaking (Collision Detection.)

---

3. The precise term as defined in the Ethernet standard is "frame," but the term "packet" is often used as well. Both terms are used in this book.

To translate this into Ethernet terms, each interface must wait until there is no signal on the channel, then it can begin transmitting. If some other interface is transmitting there will be a signal on the channel, which is called carrier. All other interfaces must wait until carrier ceases before trying to transmit, and this process is called Carrier Sense.

All Ethernet interfaces are equal in their ability to send frames onto the network. No one gets a higher priority than anyone else, and democracy reigns. This is what is meant by Multiple Access. Since signals take a finite time to travel from one end of an Ethernet system to the other, the first bits of a transmitted frame do not reach all parts of the network simultaneously. Therefore, it's possible for two interfaces to sense that the network is idle and to start transmitting their frames simultaneously. When this happens, the Ethernet system has a way to sense the "collision" of signals and to stop the transmission and resend the frames. This is called Collision Detect.

The CSMA/CD protocol is designed to provide fair access to the shared channel so that all stations get a chance to use the network. After every packet transmission all stations use the CSMA/CD protocol to determine which station gets to use the Ethernet channel next.

Collisions

If more than one station happens to transmit on the Ethernet channel at the same moment, then the signals are said to collide. The stations are notified of this event, and instantly reschedule their transmission using a specially designed backoff algorithm. As part of this algorithm the stations involved each choose a random time interval to schedule the retransmission of the frame, which keeps the stations from making transmission attempts in lock step.

It's unfortunate that the original Ethernet design used the word "collision" for this aspect of the Ethernet medium access control mechanism. If it had been called something else, such as "stochastic arbitration event (SAE)," then no one would worry about the occurrence of SAEs on an Ethernet. However, "collision" sounds like something bad has happened, leading many people to think that collisions are an indication of network failure.

The truth of the matter is that collisions are absolutely normal and expected events on an Ethernet, and simply indicate that the CSMA/CD protocol is functioning as designed. As more computers are added to a given Ethernet, and as the traffic level increases, more collisions will occur as part of the normal operation of an Ethernet.

The design of the system ensures that the majority of collisions on an Ethernet that is not overloaded will be resolved in microseconds, or millionths of a second. A normal collision does not result in lost data. In the event of a collision the Ethernet interface backs off (waits) for some number of microseconds, and then automatically retransmits the data.

On a network with heavy traffic loads it may happen that there are multiple collisions for a given frame transmission attempt. This is also normal behavior. If repeated collisions occur for a given transmission attempt, then the stations involved begin expanding the set of potential backoff times from which they chose their random retransmission time.

Repeated collisions for a given packet transmission attempt indicate a busy network. The expanding backoff process, formally known as "truncated binary exponential backoff," is a clever feature of the Ethernet MAC that provides an automatic method for stations to adjust to traffic conditions on the network. Only after 16 consecutive collisions for a given transmission attempt will the interface finally discard the Ethernet packet. This can happen only if the Ethernet channel is overloaded for a fairly long period of time, or is broken in some way.

Best Effort Data Delivery

This brings up an interesting point, which is that the Ethernet system, in common with other LAN technologies, operates as a best effort" data delivery system. To keep the complexity and cost of a LAN to a reasonable level, no guarantee of reliable data delivery is made. While the bit error rate of a LAN channel is carefully engineered to produce a system that normally delivers data extremely well, errors can still occur.

A burst of electrical noise may occur somewhere in a cabling system, for example, corrupting the data in a frame and causing it to be dropped. Or a LAN channel may become overloaded for some period of time, which in the case of Ethernet can cause 16 collisions to occur on a transmission attempt, leading to a dropped frame. No matter what technology is used, no LAN system is perfect, which is why higher protocol layers of network software are designed to recover from errors.

It is up to the high-level protocol that is sending data over the network to make sure that the data is correctly received at the destination computer. High-level network protocols can do this by establishing a reliable data transport service using sequence numbers and acknowledgment mechanisms in the packets that they send over the LAN.

1.6 Ethernet Frame and Ethernet Addresses

The heart of the Ethernet system is the Ethernet frame, which is used to deliver data between computers. The frame consists of a set of bits organized into several fields. These fields include address fields, a variable size data field that carries from 46 to 1,500 bytes of data, and an error checking field that checks the integrity of the bits in the frame to make sure that the frame has arrived intact.

The first two fields in the frame carry 48-bit addresses, called the destination and source addresses. The IEEE controls the assignment of these addresses by administering a portion of the address field. The IEEE does this by providing 24-bit identifiers called "Organizationally Unique Identifiers" (OUIs), since a unique 24-bit identifier is assigned to each organization that wishes to build Ethernet interfaces. The organization, in turn, creates 48-bit addresses using the assigned OUI as the first 24 bits of the address. This 48-bit address is also known as the physical address, hardware address, or MAC address.

A unique 48-bit address is commonly pre-assigned to each Ethernet interface when it is manufactured, which vastly simplifies the setup and operation of the network. For one thing, pre-assigned addresses keep you from getting involved in administering the addresses for different groups using the network. And if you've ever tried to get different work groups at a large site to cooperate and voluntarily obey the same set of rules, you can appreciate what an advantage this can be.

As each Ethernet frame is sent onto the shared signal channel, all Ethernet interfaces look at the first 48-bit field of the frame, which contains the destination address. The interfaces compare the destination address of the frame with their own address. The Ethernet interface with the same address as the destination address in the frame will read in the entire frame and deliver it to the networking software running on that computer. All other network interfaces will stop reading the frame when they discover that the destination address does not match their own address.

Multicast and Broadcast Addresses

A multicast address allows a single Ethernet frame to be received by a group of stations. Network software can set a station's Ethernet interface to listen for specific multicast addresses. This makes it possible for a set of stations to be assigned to a multicast group which has been given a specific multicast address. A single packet sent to the multicast address assigned to that group will then be received by all stations in that group.

There is also the special case of the multicast address known as the broadcast address, which is the 48-bit address of all ones. All Ethernet interfaces that see a frame with this destination address will read the frame in and deliver it to the networking software on the computer.

1.7 High-Level Protocols and Ethernet Addresses

Computers attached to an Ethernet can send application data to one another using high-level protocol software, such as the TCP/IP protocol suite used on the worldwide Internet. The high-level protocol packets are carried between computers in the data field of Ethernet frames. The system of high-level protocols carrying application data and the Ethernet system are independent entities that cooperate to deliver data between computers.

High-level protocols have their own system of addresses, such as the 32-bit address used in the current version of IP. The high-level IP-based networking software in a given station is aware of its own 32-bit IP address and can read the 48-bit Ethernet address of its network interface, but it doesn't know what the Ethernet addresses of other stations on the network may be.

To make things work, there needs to be some way to discover the Ethernet addresses of other IP-based stations on the network. For several high-level protocols, including TCP/IP, this is done using yet another high-level protocol called the Address Resolution Protocol (ARP). As an example of how Ethernet and one family of high-level protocols interact, let's take a quick look at how the ARP protocol functions.

Operation of the ARP Protocol

The operation of ARP is straightforward. Let's say an IP-based station (station "A") with IP address 192.0.2.1 wishes to send data over the Ethernet channel to another IP-based station (station "B") with IP address 192.0.2.2. Station "A" sends a packet to the broadcast address containing an ARP request. The ARP request basically says "Will the station on this Ethernet channel that has the IP address of 192.0.2.2 please tell me what the address of its Ethernet interface is?"

Since the ARP request is sent in a broadcast frame, every Ethernet interface on the network reads it in and hands the ARP request to the networking software running on the station. Only station "B" with IP address 192.0.2.2 will respond, by sending a packet containing the Ethernet address of station "B" back to the requesting station. Now station "A" has an Ethernet address to which it can send data destined for station "B," and the high-level protocol communication can proceed.

A given Ethernet system can carry several different kinds of high-level protocol data. For example, a single Ethernet can carry data between computers in the form of TCP/IP protocols as well as Novell or AppleTalk protocols. The Ethernet is simply a trucking system that carries packages of data between computers; it doesn't care what is inside the packages.

1.8 Signal Topology and Media System Timing

When it comes to how signals flow over the set of media segments that make up an Ethernet system, it helps to understand the topology of the system. The signal topology of the Ethernet is also known as the logical topology, to distinguish it from the actual physical layout of the media cables. The logical topology of an Ethernet provides a single channel (or bus) that carries Ethernet signals to all stations.

Multiple Ethernet segments can be linked together to form a larger Ethernet LAN using a signal amplifying and retiming device called a repeater. Through the use of repeaters, a given Ethernet system of multiple segments can grow as a "non-rooted branching tree." This means that each media segment is an individual branch of the complete signal system. Even though the media segments may be physically connected in a star pattern, with multiple segments attached to a repeater, the logical topology is still that of a single Ethernet channel that carries signals to all stations.

The notion of "tree" is just a formal name for systems like this, and a typical network design actually ends up looking more like a complex concatenation of network segments. On media segments that support multiple connections, such as coaxial Ethernet, you may install a repeater and a link to another segment at any point on the segment.

Other types of segments known as link segments can only have one connection at each end. This is described in more detail in the individual media segment chapters.

"Non-rooted" means that the resulting system of linked segments may grow in any direction, and does not have a specific root segment. Most importantly, segments must never be connected in a loop. Every segment in the system must have two ends, since the Ethernet system will not operate correctly in the presence of loop paths.

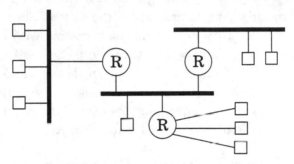

FIGURE 1.1   Ethernet signal topology

The figure shows several media segments linked with repeaters and connecting to stations. A signal sent from any station travels over that station's segment and is repeated onto all other segments. This way it is heard by all other stations over the single Ethernet channel.

As shown here, the physical topology may include bus cables or a star cable layout. The three segments connected to a single repeater are laid out in the star physical topology, for example. The point is that no matter how the media segments are physically connected together, there is one signal channel delivering frames over those segments to all stations on a given Ethernet LAN.

Round Trip Timing
In order for the media access control system to work properly, all Ethernet interfaces must be capable of responding to one another's signals within a specified amount of time. The signal timing is based on the amount of time it takes for a signal to get from one end of the

complete media system and back, which is known as the "round trip time." The maximum round trip time of signals on the shared Ethernet channel is strictly limited to ensure that every interface can hear all network signals within the specified amount of time provided in the Ethernet medium access control system.

The longer a given network segment is, the more time it takes for a signal to travel over it. The intent of the configuration guidelines is to make sure that the round trip timing limits are met, no matter what combination of media segments are used in the system. The configuration guidelines provide rules for combining segments with repeaters so that the correct signal timing is maintained for the entire LAN. If the specifications for individual media segment lengths and the configuration rules for combining segments are not followed, then computers may not hear one another's signals within the required time limit, and could end up interfering with one another.

The correct operation of an Ethernet LAN depends upon media segments that are built according to the rules published for each media type. More complex LANs built with multiple media types must be designed according to the multi-segment configuration guidelines provided in the Ethernet standard. These rules include limits on the total number of segments and repeaters that may be in a given system, to ensure that the correct round trip timing is maintained.

1.9 Extending Ethernets with Hubs

Ethernet was designed to be easily expandable to meet the networking needs of a given site. To help extend Ethernet systems, networking vendors sell devices that provide multiple Ethernet ports. These devices are known as hubs since they provide the central portion, or hub, of a media system.

There are two major kinds of hub: repeater hubs and switching hubs. As we've seen, each port of a repeater hub links individual Ethernet media segments together to create a larger network that operates as a single Ethernet LAN. The total set of segments and repeaters in the

Ethernet LAN must meet the round trip timing specifications. The second kind of hub provides packet switching, typically based on bridging ports as described in Chapter 15.

The important thing to know at this point is that each port of a packet switching hub provides a connection to an Ethernet media system that operates as a separate Ethernet LAN. Unlike a repeater hub whose individual ports combine segments together to create a single large LAN, a switching hub makes it possible to divide a set of Ethernet media systems into multiple LANs that are linked together by way of the packet switching electronics in the hub. The round trip timing rules for each LAN stop at the switching hub port. This allows you to link a large number of individual Ethernet LANs together.

A given Ethernet LAN can consist of merely a single cable segment linking some number of computers, or it may consist of a repeater hub linking several such media segments together. Whole Ethernet LANs can themselves be linked together to form extended network systems using packet switching hubs. While an individual Ethernet LAN may typically support anywhere from a few up to several dozen computers, the total system of Ethernet LANs linked with packet switches at a given site may support many hundreds or thousands of machines.

1.10 Summary

We have covered a lot of territory in this tutorial. Beginning with the invention of Ethernet and how the Ethernet standards evolved, we went on to describe the operation of the basic Ethernet system, including the Ethernet medium access control mechanism. Following that, we took a look at the collision detection and backoff mechanism, which is an essential feature of the normal operation of an Ethernet.

Next we explained the Ethernet frame and the address that is assigned to each Ethernet interface. The way in which a high-level protocol finds the Ethernet address using the ARP protocol was also briefly described.

Finally, we described the topology of Ethernet and explained why the network segments used to build an Ethernet LAN must all obey certain round trip timing restrictions. The configuration rules in the IEEE 802.3 standard show how to combine segments with repeaters to make sure that the total system of segments meets the timing requirements for an Ethernet LAN. We also noted that multiple Ethernet LANs can be linked with packet switches.

The following chapters describe the configuration rules that apply to each media variety, and the multi-segment configuration rules that allow you to combine multiple segments while still maintaining the correct signal timing.

CHAPTER 2   10-Mbps Media Systems

2.1 10-Mbps Media Systems

The CSMA/CD medium access protocol and the format of the Ethernet frame are identical for all Ethernet media varieties, no matter what speed they operate at. However, the individual 10-Mbps and 100-Mbps media varieties each use different components and have very different configuration guidelines.

The original Ethernet system operates at 10-Mbps, and there are four baseband media segments defined in the 10-Mbps Ethernet standard that are described here.

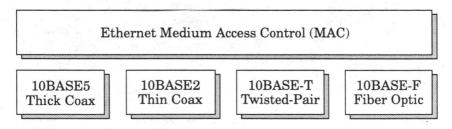

FIGURE 2.1   Four 10-Mbps Ethernet media varieties

The four media types are shown with their IEEE shorthand identifiers. The IEEE identifiers include three pieces of information. The first item, "10", stands for the media speed of 10-Mbps. The word "BASE" stands for "baseband," which is a type of signaling. Baseband signaling simply means that Ethernet signals are the only signals carried over the media system.

The third part of the identifier provides a rough indication of segment type or length. For thick coax the "5" indicates the 500 meter maximum length allowed for individual segments of thick coaxial cable. For thin coax the "2" is rounded up from the 185 meter maximum length for individual thin coaxial segments. The "T" and "F" stand for "twisted-pair" and "fiber optic," and simply indicate the cable type.

The thick coaxial media segment was the first one defined in the earliest Ethernet specifications. Next came the thin coaxial segment, followed by the twisted-pair and fiber optic media segments. The twisted-pair segment type is the most widely used today for making network connections to the desktop.

2.2 Components Used in the 10-Mbps Media System

Shown next is a block diagram of the components that can be used to make a connection to the 10-Mbps media system.

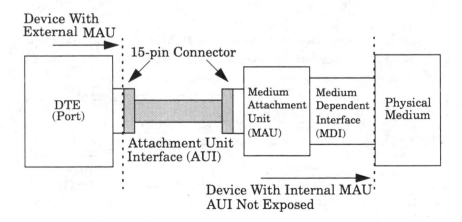

FIGURE 2.2   Block diagram of a 10-Mbps network connection

The figure shows the components defined in the IEEE standard for making an attachment to a 10-Mbps media system. While this set of entities and their three-letter identifiers might seem like more alphabet soup of interest to network engineers only, these identifiers describe real-world devices that you need to know about. We use the three-letter acronyms from the standard since you will find them used in vendor literature and printed on Ethernet devices.

Physical Medium

On the right hand side of the block diagram in the figure is the physical medium, which is used to carry Ethernet signals among computers. As we've just seen, this could be any one of several 10-Mbps media types including thick or thin coaxial cable, twisted-pair cable, and fiber optic cable.

Medium Dependent Interface

The connection to the medium is made with something called the medium dependent interface, or MDI. In the real world, this is a piece of hardware used for making a direct physical and electrical connection to the network cable. In the case of thick coaxial Ethernet, the most commonly used MDI is a type of clamp that is installed directly onto the coaxial cable. For twisted-pair Ethernet, the MDI is an eight-pin connector, which is also referred to as an RJ-45 telephone-style jack. The eight-pin jack provides a connection to the four twisted-pair wires used to carry network signals in the 10-Mbps twisted-pair media system.

Medium Attachment Unit

The next device in the block diagram is called the medium attachment unit, or MAU. This device is called a transceiver in the original DIX Ethernet standard, since it both TRANSmits and reCEIVEs signals on the medium. The medium dependent interface just mentioned is actually a part of the MAU, and provides the MAU with a direct physical and electrical connection to the medium.

Attachment Unit Interface

To the left of the MAU in the block diagram is the attachment unit interface or AUI. This is called a transceiver cable in the DIX standard. The AUI provides a path for signals and power carried between the Ethernet interface and the MAU. The AUI may be connected to the Ethernet interface in the computer with a 15-pin connector.

Data Terminal Equipment, or Computer

The networked device itself is defined as data terminal equipment (DTE) in the IEEE standard. Each DTE attached to an Ethernet is equipped with an Ethernet interface. The Ethernet interface provides a connection to the Ethernet media system and contains the electronics and software needed to perform the medium access control functions required to send a frame over the Ethernet channel.

Note that Ethernet ports on repeaters do not use an Ethernet interface. A repeater port connects to the Ethernet media system using the same AUI, MAU, and MDI equipment. However, repeater ports operate at the individual bit level for Ethernet signals, moving the signals directly from segment to segment. Therefore, repeater ports do not use Ethernet interfaces to perform their function, since they do not operate at the level of Ethernet frames.

On the other hand, a repeater hub may be equipped with an Ethernet interface to provide a way to communicate with the hub over the network. This allows the vendor to provide a management interface in the hub that can interact with a remote management station, using the Simple Network Management Protocol (SNMP). Managed hubs make it possible for a network manager to remotely monitor the traffic levels and error conditions on hub ports, to shut off ports for troubleshooting, etc.

2.3 Putting it All Together

And there we have it: for a typical station connection the DTE (computer) contains an Ethernet interface which forms up and sends Ethernet frames that carry data between computers attached to the network. The Ethernet interface is attached to the media system using a set of equipment that can include an AUI (transceiver cable) and a MAU (transceiver) with its associated MDI (coaxial cable clamp, twisted-pair RJ45-style jack, etc.).

The MAU and MDI are specifically designed for each media type used in Ethernet. Coaxial MAUs differ from twisted-pair MAUs, for example, both in the technology used for the actual connection to the media (the MDI), as well as the method used for sending Ethernet signals over the media and for detecting collisions.

2.4 Internal and External MAUs

Notice that in the figure above there are dashed lines indicating the two kinds of configurations shown – one with an external MAU and one with an internal MAU. With an external configuration a DTE or repeater port is equipped with a 15-pin AUI connector. The AUI cable and MAU are both located outside the device. This is how a computer or repeater looks when connected to an Ethernet segment using an external transceiver cable and external transceiver.

However, it's also possible for the MAU and AUI to be integrated as part of the electronics inside the DTE or repeater port. In this case, the only exposed device on the device is the MDI that connects directly to the network media. This is the type of connection found on a thin coax or twisted-pair Ethernet interface used in a DTE, for example.

CHAPTER 3 10-Mbps Thick Coax, Type 10BASE5

3.1 10-Mbps Thick Coaxial Media System

The thick coaxial media system was the first media system specified in the original Ethernet standard of 1980. Today most sites use twisted-pair media for connections to the desktop.

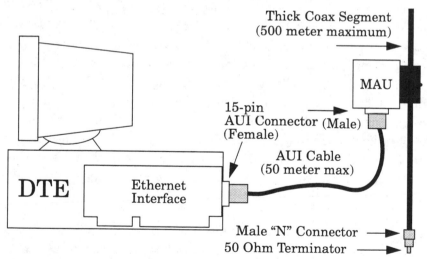

FIGURE 3.1   Connecting a computer to thick Ethernet

Thick coaxial segments are still sometimes installed as a backbone segment for interconnecting Ethernet hubs, since thick coaxial media provides a low-cost cable with good electrical shielding that can carry signals relatively long distances between hubs.

On the other hand, thick coaxial cable is limited to carrying 10-Mbps signals only, which means you must replace the cable if you wish to link hubs together at higher speeds. High quality twisted-pair cable or fiber optic cable can carry either 10-Mbps or 100-Mbps signals, therefore many sites prefer to use these cables as a way of linking hubs together.

3.2 10BASE5 Components

The following set of five components are used to build a thick coaxial segment and to make connections to it. It should be emphasized that this is just a quick introduction and brief survey that does not provide the detailed information you need to construct and manage media systems.

Network Medium

The thick Ethernet segment is based on a thick (approx 1 cm or 0.4 inch diameter) and relatively inflexible coaxial cable. The outer insulation (jacket) of the cable may be plain PVC (yellow color) or Teflon (orange-brown color). Teflon is used for "plenum rated" cable, which is often required for installation in air handling spaces (also called plenums) to meet fire regulations. Thick Ethernet coaxial cable must be designed especially for use in Ethernet systems so that it meets the specifications, including a 50 ohms characteristic impedance rating and a solid center conductor. Examples of thick coaxial cables specifically designed for Ethernet are Belden numbers 9880 (PVC) and 89880 (plenum rated).

Thick coaxial segments are equipped with male type "N" coaxial connectors at each end. Installing the coaxial connectors onto the cable requires special stripping and crimping tools and must be done carefully or signal problems may result. For this reason, the correct operation of thick coaxial segments depends very much on the correct installation of the coaxial connectors.

The specifications note that the thick coaxial segment should ideally be built using a single piece of cable from the same cable spool or from cable spools all manufactured at the same time (known as a cable lot). If cable from different lots is used to build up a thick coax segment, then the specifications note that the sections of cable used should be 23.4 meters, 70.2 meters, or 117 meters in length (all lengths may be +/- 0.5 meters). The reason for using these lengths of cable is to minimize the chance of having excessive signal reflections build up due to the slight variations in electrical characteristics that can occur between different cable manufacturers or cable lots.

Terminator and Grounding

There must be a type N 50 ohm terminator installed at each end of a thick coaxial cable segment. The standard notes that the thick coax segment should be grounded at one point for electrical safety reasons. There must only be one grounding point, to avoid disrupting the Ethernet signals carried by the cable. All other metal parts on the cable should be insulated or carefully routed and fastened in place with plastic cable ties to avoid accidentally touching an electrical ground.

MAU (Transceiver)

An Ethernet interface is attached to a thick Ethernet segment with an external MAU. The MAU provides an electrical connection to the thick Ethernet coax and transfers signals between the Ethernet interface and the network segment.

The specifications state that there may be a maximum of 100 MAUs attached to a segment, and that each MAU connection to the thick coax be placed on any one of the black bands marked on the coaxial cable. The black bands printed on thick coaxial cable provide connection points that are spaced a minimum of 2.5 meters apart. The minimum spacing and the restriction on the number of MAUs are both designed to limit the amount of signal attenuation and distortion that can occur on a given cable segment.

The most popular attachment mechanism (MDI) for a 10BASE5 MAU is sold by AMP Corporation, and consists of a metal and plastic clamp that makes a direct physical and electrical connection to the coaxial cable. This clamp is also called a transceiver tap, since to install the clamp you must drill a hole into the thick coaxial cable in a process known as tapping the cable. Since this clamp may be installed while the network is active, it is also called a "non-intrusive" tap.

Another, much less popular, form of thick Ethernet MDI consists of a tap composed of two type N coaxial cable connectors. Installing this tap requires cutting the thick coaxial cable, installing N connectors on each cable end, and then installing the tap as a type of "barrel" connector in-line with the coaxial cable. Cutting the cable halts the operation of the network, earning this approach the label of "intrusive tap."

The external MAU is equipped with a male 15-pin AUI connector that has two locking posts, providing an attachment point for a sliding latch connector. The MAU is powered from the Ethernet interface. The specifications state that a MAU may draw as much as 0.5 AMP (1/2 AMP) of 12 volt DC power.

AUI Cable (Transceiver Cable)

An AUI cable can be used to provide the connection between an external MAU and the Ethernet interface. The MAU is equipped with a male 15-pin connector with locking posts, and the Ethernet interface (DTE) is equipped with a female 15-pin connector that is typically provided with a sliding latch.[1]

The AUI cable, in turn, has a female 15-pin connector on one end that is equipped with a sliding latch; this is the end that is attached to the MAU. The other end of the AUI cable has a male 15-pin connector that is typically equipped with locking posts; this is the end that is attached to the Ethernet interface. Some 15-pin connectors on Ethernet interfaces are equipped with screw posts instead of the sliding

---

1. The sliding latch connector is probably the least-liked part of the Ethernet standard, due to the ease with which poorly constructed and installed versions of these connectors can become loose and fall off. Vendors have improved the design and construction of the sliding latch over the years, so that recent connectors tend to work better.

latch fastener described in the standard, requiring a special AUI cable with locking screws on one end instead of sliding latch posts.

A transceiver cable is built like an electrical extension cord; there's a plug (male connector) on one end, and a socket (female connector) on the other end. If you needed to, you could connect several AUI cables together to reach between an interface and a MAU. This is not recommended, however, since the sliding latch connectors may not hold the cable ends together very well.

The AUI cable carries three data signals between the Ethernet interface and MAU: transmit data (from the Ethernet interface to the network), receive data (from the network to the interface), and a collision presence signal (from the network to the interface). Each signal is sent over a pair of wires. Another pair of wires are used to carry 12 volt DC power from the Ethernet interface to the MAU.

The standard AUI cable is relatively thick (approx. 1cm or 0.4 inch diameter), and may be up to 50 meters (164 feet) long. "Office grade" AUI cables are available that are thinner and more flexible. The thinner wires used in office grade AUI cables also have higher signal loss than the wires in standard AUI cables, which limits the length of office grade cables. One vendor of office grade cables rates them as having four times the amount of signal attenuation as standard cables, and only sells them in two and five meter lengths. The maximum allowable length between a station and a MAU for these office grade AUI cables is 12.5 meters (41 feet).

Ethernet Interface

An Ethernet interface may be an adapter board that is installed in the computer, or may be built into the computer at the factory. To provide an attachment to a thick coaxial segment, an Ethernet interface is typically equipped with a female 15-pin connector and sliding latch for an AUI cable attachment. Some interfaces may use non-standard AUI connectors as described in Chapter 8.

3.3 10BASE5 Configuration Guidelines

The following table lists the guidelines for a single segment of 10BASE5 thick coaxial cable.

TABLE 3.1 10BASE5 segment configuration guidelines

Maximum Segment Length		Maximum Number of MAUs	
Thick Coax 10BASE5	500 m (1640 ft.)	Per 10BASE5 Segment	100
AUI	50 m (164 ft.)		

The five components described in this chapter are all that's needed to build a single thick Ethernet cable segment with a maximum length of 500 meters, which can support up to 100 MAU attachments.

If you wish to combine multiple segments, the multi-segment configuration rules in the IEEE standard require that the media segments be connected together with Ethernet repeaters. A repeater is a signal amplifying and retiming device that keeps the system operating correctly by cleaning up the signals that it repeats from one segment to the other. The repeater also has circuits that ensure that collision signals that occur on any segment are propagated onto all other segments to which the repeater is attached.

By doing this the repeater makes all segments function as though they were a single big segment, or what is known as a single Ethernet "collision domain." This makes it possible for computers attached to any segment in a system of Ethernet segments linked with repeaters to hear the same signals and to operate as a single LAN channel.

A thick coaxial segment is formally known as a "mixing segment" in the multi-segment configuration guidelines. A mixing segment is defined as one which may have more than two MDI connections. As we've just seen, a given segment of thick coaxial cable can support up to 100 such connections. This distinguishes it from a link segment, which has only one connection at each end.

3.4 Thick Coaxial Physical Topology

In Chapter 1 we saw that the logical topology of an Ethernet signal-ling system is a non-rooted branching tree, which describes how seg-ments may be connected together. There is also a physical topology for each segment type, which describes how each segment type used in an Ethernet system can be physically connected to stations.

Thick coaxial segments can only be connected in the bus cable form of physical topology. In the bus cable topology, all stations are attached to a single coaxial cable that provides an electrical signal bus that is common to all stations and carries signals between all stations.

FIGURE 3.2   Thick Ethernet bus cable topology

One problem with the bus cabling topology is that a failure anywhere on the thick coaxial cable disrupts the electrical bus and therefore dis-rupts the operation of all computers attached to the cable. A star-wired cabling topology can make it much easier to limit the effect of cabling problems, as shown in the next several chapters.

CHAPTER 4 10-Mbps Thin Coax, Type 10BASE2

4.1 10-Mbps Thin Coaxial Media System

The thin coaxial Ethernet system uses a much more flexible cable that makes it possible to connect the coaxial cable directly to the Ethernet interface in the computer. This results in a lower-cost and easier to use system that was popular for desktop connections until the twisted-pair media system was developed.

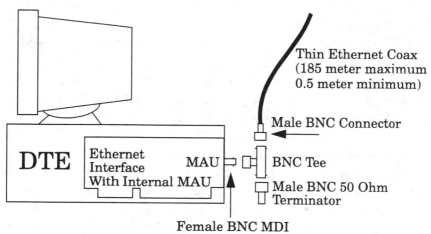

FIGURE 4.1   Connecting a computer to thin Ethernet

In the thin coaxial system the AUI, MAU, and MDI are part of the network interface in the computer. This reduces the number of outboard components you need to purchase and install to connect a computer to the medium, thereby lowering the cost of an attachment to the network.

The flexibility and low cost of the thin coaxial system continues to make it popular for networking clusters of workstations in an open lab setting, for example. However, like the thick coaxial system, thin coax is limited to carrying 10-Mbps signals only.

4.2 10BASE2 Components

The following components are used to build a thin coaxial Ethernet segment and to make connections to it. It should be emphasized that this is just an introduction and brief survey that does not provide the detailed information you need to construct and manage media systems.

Network Medium

The thin Ethernet system is based on thinner (approximately 0.5 cm or 3/16th of an inch) coaxial cable that is more flexible and easier to deal with than the thick Ethernet variety. The cable must have a 50 ohm characteristic impedance rating, and a stranded center conductor. These specifications may be met by cable types RG 58 A/U or RG 58 C/U, but cable vendors sometimes use these cable numbers for cables with different impedance ratings. It's up to you to make sure that the cable you purchase meets the media specifications.

One way to do this is by using cable specifically designed and rated by the cable vendor for use as thin Ethernet coax. Thin Ethernet cable sections must be equipped with male BNC-type connectors at each end. BNC connectors are lower cost and easier to install than the N-connectors used on thick coaxial cables.

Terminators and grounding

Each end of a complete thin Ethernet segment must be equipped with a 50 ohm terminating resistance. Multiport repeaters used for linking thin Ethernet segments often have internal 50 ohm termination provided on each port, which eases the task of terminating the end of the thin coax segment attached to the repeater. Some thin Ethernet repeaters have switchable termination that you can enable or disable, depending on your requirements. It is essential that exactly two 50 ohm terminators be installed or enabled on a given segment, or the collision detection mechanism in the MAUs attached to the segment will not function correctly.

The standard notes that you may provide a thin coaxial segment with a grounding point for electrical safety. To avoid disrupting the Ethernet signals carried by the cable, there must only be one grounding point. All other metal parts on the cable should be insulated or carefully routed and fastened in place with plastic cable ties to avoid accidentally touching an electrical ground.

Interface and MAU

In the thin Ethernet system the MAU is built into the Ethernet interface, and therefore an external AUI cable is not required. The thin coax is flexible enough to be connected directly to the female BNC connector on the interface. To make an attachment to a thin Ethernet segment, the female BNC connector is attached to one end of a BNC Tee connector, so called because it is shaped like the letter "T." The other two ends of the BNC Tee make a physical and electrical connection to the thin Ethernet segment.

To help make the individual pieces clearer, the BNC connectors in Figure 4.1 are shown unattached to one another. The thin Ethernet segment in the figure is drawn as terminating at this computer to show you how a thin Ethernet terminator is connected.

4.3 10BASE2 Configuration Guidelines

Thin coax segments may be a maximum of 185 meters in length, and not 200 meters as the rounded-up "2" in the shorthand identifier might lead you to believe.

TABLE 4.1 10BASE2 segment configuration guidelines

Maximum Segment Length		Maximum Number of MAUs	
Thin Coax 10BASE2	185 m (606.9 ft.)	Per 10BASE2 Segment	30

The thin Ethernet coaxial segment is defined as a mixing segment, since it can support more than two MDI connections. Up to 30 MAUs are allowed on each thin Ethernet segment. The standard requires that multiple segments of thin coaxial cable be linked with repeaters. Each repeater connection requires a MAU that must be counted toward the total of 30 MAU connections per segment.

Thin Coaxial Segment Length

Since thin coaxial cable has higher resistance than thick coax, the limit of 185 meters of cable helps ensure that losses are held to acceptable limits. The standard also recommends using high quality BNC connectors with low resistance gold plated center conductors. The limit on the number of connections and the recommendation of low resistance connectors is intended to help reduce the DC (direct current) resistance caused by the coaxial connectors used in a thin Ethernet system. This, in turn, helps ensure that the total DC resistance of the segment is kept low enough so that the essential collision detect mechanism continues to work properly.

There are no special MAU spacing rules in the thin Ethernet media system. However, the specifications state that the pieces of coaxial cable used to build a thin Ethernet segment may be no shorter than 0.5 meters (1.64 feet) in length. This effectively sets the minimum spacing between MAU connections to 0.5 meters.

4.4 Thin Coaxial Physical Topology

A given thin Ethernet segment may be connected to several computers in a topology known as "daisy chaining." In the daisy chain topology a piece of thin coax is connected to the BNC Tee, instead of a terminator; this piece of coax is then attached to the BNC Tee on the next computer in line. The BNC Tee at the very end of the segment is the only one that should have a terminator.

Figure 4.2 shows two cable topologies that thin coaxial cable supports. A two-port repeater is shown connecting two thin coax segments. One of the thin coaxial segments is shown in the daisy chain topology, connected to DTEs 1, 2, and 3. By connecting the short cable pieces and BNC connectors together, you create the complete segment, which can link up to 29 stations and one repeater port, for a total of 30 MAU connections.

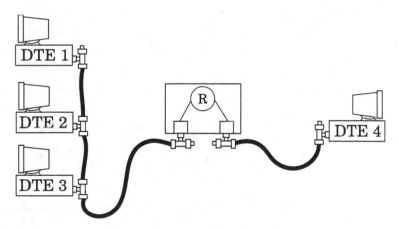

FIGURE 4.2   Thin Ethernet cable topologies

In the daisy chain topology, if anyone incorrectly removes a thin Ethernet coax segment from the BNC Tee connector on the back of their computer, the entire segment will stop working for all other computers. Removing the entire BNC Tee connector from the female BNC on the Ethernet interface will not disrupt the segment, however, since the entire length of the coaxial cable continues to function in that case.

The other segment is shown connected directly to one computer, DTE 4, and then terminating. This point-to-point segment supports only one computer, which limits the number of computers that can be affected by cable problems to the single machine on that segment.

Thin Coaxial Cable Stubs

Note that the BNC Tee is connected directly to the female BNC on the interface, with no intervening piece of thin coaxial cable. The standard notes that the length of the "stub" connection from the BNC MDI on the interface to the coaxial cable should be no longer than four centimeters (1.57 inches), to prevent the occurrence of signal reflections which can cause frame errors.

While longer stub cables inserted between the BNC Tee and the Ethernet interface may seem to work, they actually create signal reflections which cause electrical noise and result in frame errors. Frames lost due to frame errors are typically detected and retransmitted by the application software. Therefore, the system may appear to work when stubs are used since a small level of frame loss is not usually noticed right away.

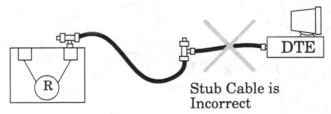

Stub Cable is Incorrect

FIGURE 4.3   Thin coax stub cable is incorrect

However, a large enough frame error rate can cause a high number of retransmissions and make the network appear to slow down. The electrical noise and frame loss get worse as the traffic level increases, causing the response time of applications over the network to plummet just when the demand is highest. You can avoid these problems by making sure that there are no stub cables in your thin Ethernet system.

CHAPTER 5   10-Mbps Twisted-Pair,
Type 10BASE-T

5.1 10-Mbps Twisted-Pair Media System

The "T" in 10BASE-T stands for "twisted" in reference to the twisted-pair wire used for this variety of Ethernet.

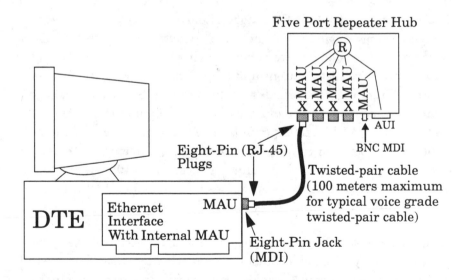

FIGURE 5.1   Connecting a computer to twisted-pair Ethernet

The specifications for the twisted-pair media system were published in 1990. This system has since become the most widely used medium for connections to the desktop.

The 10BASE-T system operates over two pairs of wires, one pair used for receive data signals and the other pair used for transmit data signals. The two wires in each pair must be twisted together for the entire length of the segment, a standard technique used to improve the signal carrying characteristics of a wire pair. Multiple twisted-pair segments communicate by way of a multiport hub. A five-port repeater hub is shown in the figure.

5.2 10BASE-T Components

The following set of components is used to build a 10BASE-T segment and to make connections to it. It should be emphasized that this is just an introduction and brief survey that does not provide the detailed information you need to construct and manage media systems.

Network Medium

The 10 Mbps twisted-pair Ethernet system was designed to allow segments of approximately 100 meters in length when using modern "voice grade" twisted-pair telephone wiring that meets the EIA/TIA Category 3[1] wire specifications and follows the correct wiring scheme. The maximum segment length at your site may be shorter or longer than this depending on the quality of the twisted-pair cabling in your system. The EIA/TIA cabling standard recommends a segment length of 90 meters between the wire termination equipment in the wiring closet, and the wall plate in the office. This provides 10 meters of cable allowance to accommodate patch cables at each end of the link, signal losses in intermediate wire terminations on the link, etc.

While the 10BASE-T system is designed to use voice grade telephone cable that may already be installed, many sites choose to install higher quality Category 5 cables, connectors, and wire terminating devices to provide data service to the desktop. These higher quality components work well for 10BASE-T and also provide the best possible signal carrying system for the 100-Mbps Ethernet media systems.

---

1. The EIA/TIA wire categories are described in Appendix C.

This approach makes it a relatively straightforward task to increase the bandwidth of your network system when it becomes necessary to accommodate increased network traffic.

There are twisted-pair Ethernet cable testers available that allow you to check the electrical characteristics of the cable you use, to see if it meets the important electrical specifications. These specifications include signal crosstalk, which is the amount of signal that crosses over between the receive and transmit pairs, and signal attenuation, which is the amount of signal loss encountered on the segment.

The 10BASE-T media system uses two pairs of wires, which are terminated in an eight-pin (RJ-45 style) connector. This means that four pins of the eight-pin MDI connector are used.

TABLE 5.1 10BASE-T eight-pin connector signals

Pin Number	Signal
1	TD+
2	TD–
3	RD+
4	Unused
5	Unused
6	RD–
7	Unused
8	Unused

The transmit and receive data signals on each pair of a 10BASE-T segment are polarized, with one wire of each signal pair carrying the positive (+) signal, and the other carrying the negative (–) signal.

While an eight-pin connector is specified in the standard for making connections to a 10BASE-T segment, you will also see 50-pin connectors used on some 10BASE-T hubs. The 50-pin connector, also called a "Telco" connector, is designed to support the voice grade wire in common use in the telephone industry, and provides a more compact way to connect a set of twisted-pair wires to a 10BASE-T hub.

10BASE-T Crossover Wiring

When connecting two twisted-pair MAUs together over a segment, the transmit data pins of one eight-pin connector must be wired to the receive data pins of the other, and vice versa. The crossover wiring may be accomplished in two ways: with a special cable or inside the hub.

For a single segment connecting only two computers you can provide the signal crossover by building a special crossover cable, with the transmit pins on the eight-pin plug at one end of the cable wired to the receive data pins on the eight-pin plug at the other end of the cross-over cable and vice versa.

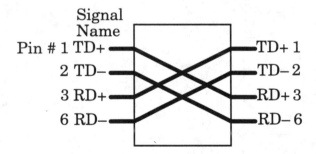

FIGURE 5.2   10BASE-T crossover cable

However, when you are wiring multiple segments in a building it's much easier to wire the cable connectors "straight through," and not worry about whether the wires in the jumper cables or other twisted-pair cables in your building have been correctly crossed over. The way to accomplish this is to do all the crossover wiring at one point in the system: inside the multiport hub.

The standard recommends that the signal crossover be done internally in each hub port. If the crossover function is done inside a hub port, then the standard notes that the port should be marked with an "X."

10BASE-T Link Integrity Test

10BASE-T MAUs continually monitor the receive data path for activity as a means of checking that the link is working correctly. When the network is idle, the MAUs also send a link test signal to one another to verify link integrity. Vendors can optionally provide a link light on the MAU; if the link lights on both MAUs are lit when you connect a segment, then you have an indication that the segment is wired correctly.

It's important that both link lights, one at each end, be lit. That indicates that there is a correctly wired signal path between both devices. On the other hand, the presence of the link lights merely means that the segment is correctly wired. Since the link test pulse operates more slowly than actual Ethernet signals, the link lights are not always a guarantee that Ethernet signals will work over the segment. Odds are good that a correctly wired segment will work, but if the signal crosstalk on the segment is too high, then it may not work despite the presence of the link lights.

Twisted-Pair Patch Cables

A common error when connecting a computer to a twisted-pair segment is to make the connection with the widely available "silver satin" patch cable typically used to connect telephones to a telephone jack. The problem is that the typical silver satin patch cable used for telephones does not have twisted wire pairs in it. This lack of twisted pairs results in excessive signal crosstalk and can cause "phantom collisions." This occurs because collisions are detected in twisted-pair Ethernet by the simultaneous occurrence of signals on the transmit and receive wire pairs. Excessive crosstalk signals can look like simultaneous traffic and can falsely trigger the collision detect circuit.

This can result in "late collisions," which are collisions that occur too late in the transmission of an Ethernet frame. A normal collision results in the immediate retransmission of a frame by the Ethernet interface. However, a late collision results in a lost frame that must be detected and retransmitted by the application software. Retransmission by the application is a lot slower and can lead to a severe loss of application performance over the network. This problem can be avoided by using only twisted-pair patch cables rated for use in twisted-pair Ethernet systems.

5.3 10BASE-T Configuration Guidelines

10BASE-T Ethernet segments are defined as link segments in the Ethernet specifications. A link segment is formally defined as a point-to-point medium that connects two and only two MDIs. In other words, a link segment that fully complies with the IEEE 802.3 specifications has only two devices attached to it, one at each end.

TABLE 5.2 10BASE-T segment configuration guidelines

Maximum Segment Length		Maximum Number of MAUs	
Twisted-Pair 10BASE-T	100 m (328 ft.)[a]	Per Link Segment	2

a. 10BASE-T segments may be longer while still meeting the electrical specifications, depending on the quality of the twisted-pair segment.

The smallest network built with a link segment would consist of two computers, one at each end of the link segment. The more typical installation uses multiport repeaters, also called hubs, to provide a connection between a larger number of link segments.

You connect the 10BASE-T MAU in the Ethernet interface in your computer to one end of the link segment, and the other end of the link segment is connected to the MAU in the hub. That way you can attach as many link segments with their associated computers as you have hub ports, and the computers all communicate via the hub.

5.4 10BASE-T Twisted-Pair Physical Topology

The physical topology supported by twisted-pair link segments is the star. In this topology a set of link segments are connected to a hub, and radiate out from the hub to the computers like the rays from a star. Another way to visualize the topology is a wagon wheel, with the hub at the center and each link segment as a spoke of the wheel.

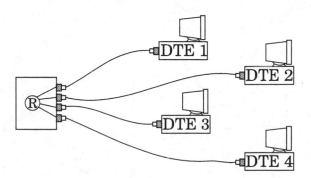

FIGURE 5.3   10BASE-T twisted-pair star topology

Figure 5.3 shows a four-port twisted-pair repeater linking four DTEs with twisted-pair link segments. The signals from each DTE are sent through the repeater, and repeated out onto all other segments.

CHAPTER 6   10-Mbps Fiber Optic, Type 10BASE-F

6.1 10-Mbps Fiber Optic Media System

The 10BASE-F fiber optic media system uses pulses of light instead of electrical currents to send signals.

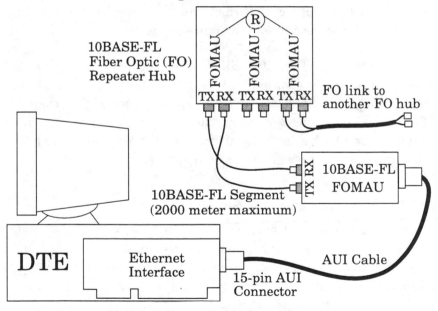

FIGURE 6.1   Connecting a computer to a 10BASE-FL segment

The use of light pulses provides superior electrical isolation for equipment at each end of a fiber link. While Ethernet equipment used in metallic media segments has protection circuits designed for typical indoor electrical hazards, fiber optic media is totally non-conductive. This complete electrical isolation provides immunity from much larger electrical hazards including the effect of lightning strikes, and from the different levels of electrical ground currents that can be found in separate buildings. Complete electrical isolation is essential when Ethernet segments must travel outside a building to link separate buildings.

The figure shows a computer linked to a repeater hub with a 10BASE-FL segment. The computer is equipped with an Ethernet interface that has a 15-pin AUI connector. This connector allows a connection to an outboard fiber optic MAU (FOMAU), using a standard AUI cable. The FOMAU, in turn, is connected to the repeater hub with two strands of fiber optic cable. Another port on the repeater is shown connecting to a fiber optic cable, which might connect to another fiber optic repeater hub located some distance away.

A major advantage of the 10BASE-FL fiber optic link segment is the long distances that it can span. Another major advantage is that fiber optic media can support transmission speeds much higher than 10-Mbps. When designing a network backbone you can use fiber optic media to link 10-Mbps hubs and upgrade to 100-Mbps hubs later. The same fiber optic media will handle both speeds.

6.2 Old and New Fiber Link Segments

The most commonly used fiber optic medium type is the link segment. There are two fiber optic link segments in use, the original Fiber Optic Inter-Repeater Link (FOIRL) segment, and the newer 10BASE-FL segment.

The original FOIRL specification from the Ethernet standard of the early 1980s provided a link segment of up to 1000 meters between two repeaters only. As the cost of repeaters dropped and more and more multiport repeater hubs were used, it became cost-effective to link individual computers to a fiber optic port on a repeater hub. Vendors created outboard FOIRL MAUs to allow this, although a repeater-to-DTE fiber connection was not specifically described in the FOIRL standard.

To deal with this and other aspects of fiber optic Ethernet, a set of fiber optic media standards, called 10BASE-F, was developed. This set of fiber standards includes revised specifications for a fiber optic link segment that allow direct attachments to computers. The full set of 10BASE-F specifications includes three segment types:

- 10BASE-FL. The 10BASE-FL standard replaces the older FOIRL specifications, and is designed to interoperate with existing FOIRL-based equipment. 10BASE-FL provides a fiber optic link segment that may be up to 2000 meters long, providing that only 10BASE-FL equipment is used in the segment. If 10BASE-FL equipment is mixed with FOIRL equipment, then the maximum segment length may be 1000 meters.

  A 10BASE-FL segment may be attached between two computers, or two repeaters, or between a computer and a repeater port. Because of the widespread use of fiber links, 10BASE-FL is the most widely used portion of the 10BASE-F fiber optic specifications, and equipment is available from a large number of vendors.

- 10BASE-FB. The 10BASE-FB specifications describe a synchronous signaling backbone segment that allows the limit on the number of repeaters that may be used in a given 10-Mbps Ethernet system to be exceeded. 10BASE-FB links typically attach to repeater hubs, and are used to link special 10BASE-FB synchronous signalling repeater hubs together in a repeated backbone system that can span long distances. Individual 10BASE-FB links may be up to 2000 meters in length. This system has a limited market and equipment is available from only a few vendors.

- 10BASE-FP. The Fiber Passive system provides a set of specifications for a fiber optic mixing segment that links multiple computers on a fiber optic media system without using repeaters. 10BASE-FP segments may be up to 500 meters long, and a single 10BASE-FP fiber optic passive star coupler may link up to 33 computers. This system has not been widely adopted and equipment does not appear to be generally available.

6.3 10BASE-FL Components

This chapter describes only the 10BASE-FL fiber link segment and the older FOIRL segment, since fiber link segments are by far the most widely used fiber optic segments in Ethernet systems today. The following components are specified for use in building a 10BASE-FL segment and making connections to it. It should be emphasized that this is just a quick introduction and brief survey that does not provide the detailed information you need to construct and manage media systems.

Network Medium
The typical fiber optic cable used for a fiber link segment is a multimode fiber cable (MMF) with a 62.5 micron fiber optic core and 125 micron outer cladding (62.5/125). Each link segment requires two strands of fiber, one to transmit data, and one to receive data. There are many kinds of fiber optic cables available, ranging from simple two-strand jumper cables with a PVC outer jacket material on up to large inter-building cables carrying many fibers in a bundle.

The fiber connectors used on link segments are generally known as "ST" connectors. The formal name of this connector in the ISO/IEC international standards is "BFOC/2.5." The ST connector is a spring-loaded bayonet connector, whose outer ring locks onto the connection, much like the BNC connector used on 10BASE2 segments. The ST connector has a key on an inner sleeve and also an outer bayonet ring. To make a connection you line up the key on the inner sleeve of the ST plug with a corresponding slot on the ST receptacle, then push the connector in and lock it in place by twisting the outer bayonet ring. This provides a tight connection with precise alignment between the two pieces of fiber optic cable being joined.

The wavelength of light used on a fiber link segment is 850 nanometers (850 nm), and the optical loss budget for a fiber link segment must be no greater than 12.5 dB. The loss budget refers to the amount of optical power lost through the attenuation of the fiber optic cable, and the inevitable small losses that occur at each fiber connector.

The more connectors you have and the longer your fiber link cable is, the higher the optical loss will be. Optical loss is measured with fiber optic test instruments that can tell you exactly how much optical loss there may be on a given segment at a given wavelength of light. A standard grade fiber optic cable operating at 850 nm will have something in the neighborhood of from 4 dB to 5 dB loss per 1000 meters. You can also expect something in the neighborhood of from 0.5 to around 2.0 dB loss per connection point, depending on how well the connection has been made. If your connectors or fiber splices are poorly made, or if there is finger oil or dust on the connector ends, then you can have higher optical loss on the segment.

The older FOIRL segment typically used the same type of fiber optic cable, connectors, and had the same optical loss budget. The 10BASE-FL specifications were designed to allow backward compatibility with existing FOIRL segments. The major difference is that the 10BASE-FL segment may be up to 2000 meters in length if only 10BASE-FL equipment is used on the segment.

10BASE-FL Link Integrity Test

10BASE-FL MAUs and older FOIRL MAUs monitor the light level on a fiber optic link segment, to provide a link integrity test. Vendors can optionally provide a link light on the MAU to give you a visual indication of the link integrity status. If the link lights on the MAUs at each end of the link are lit when you connect a MAU to the segment, then you have an indication that the segment is connected correctly and that the optical loss is within acceptable limits. If the light level drops below that required for reliable data reception, the MAU will detect this condition and stop sending or receiving data over the link.

6.4 10BASE-FL and FOIRL Configuration Guidelines

10BASE-FL and the older FOIRL segments are defined as link segments in the Ethernet specifications. A link segment is formally defined as a point-to-point medium that connects two and only two MDIs.

TABLE 6.1 Fiber link segment configuration guidelines

Maximum Segment Length		Maximum Number of MAUs	
10BASE-FL	2000 m (6561 ft.)[a]	10BASE-FL Segment	2
FOIRL	1000 m (3280 ft.)	FOIRL Segment	2

a. If 10BASE-FL MAUs are used at each end of the segment, then the segment may be up to 2000m. If one end of the segment uses an FOIRL MAU, then the segment may only be a maximum of 1000m.

The smallest network built with a link segment would consist of two computers, one at each end of the link segment. The more typical installation uses multiport repeaters, also called hubs, to provide a connection between a larger number of link segments.

6.5 Fiber Optic Link Physical Topology

The physical topology supported by fiber optic link segments is the star. In this topology a set of link segments are connected to a hub, radiating out from the hub to the computers like the rays from a star. Another way to visualize the topology is as a wagon wheel, with the hub at the center and each link segment as a spoke of the wheel. The star topology is shown in Figure 5.3.

CHAPTER 7 10-Mbps Multi-Segment Configuration Guidelines

7.1 10-Mbps Multi-Segment Configuration Guidelines

This chapter describes the rules for combining multiple segments to build larger 10-Mbps Ethernets. The IEEE 802.3 standard provides two models for verifying the configuration of multi-segment 10-Mbps baseband Ethernets. Transmission System Model 1 provides a set of "canned" configuration rules. If your network system meets these rules, then it will function correctly in terms of the essential round trip signal timing. Transmission System Model 2 provides a set of calculation aids to make it possible for you to evaluate more complex network topologies that aren't covered under the set of canned configuration rules.

We begin by looking at the scope of the configuration guidelines, to help make it clear that the guidelines apply to a single LAN. To do that, we first need to describe the function of a collision domain. Following that, we describe the Model 1 and Model 2 rules.

7.2 Scope of the Configuration Guidelines

The configuration guidelines only apply to Ethernet equipment that is built according to the IEEE 802.3 standard, and to Ethernet media systems that follow the recommendations in the standard. If your network system includes Ethernet equipment that does not fully comply with the standard, for example, you may not be able to use the configuration guidelines to verify its operation.

The reason for this is obvious when you consider that the IEEE engineers develop the configuration rules based on the known signal timing and electrical performance specifications of Ethernet equipment that fully conforms to the published standard. That way, the IEEE engineers can predict what the behavior of the Ethernet equipment will be, and how the signal timing will function across multiple segments.

If you use non-compliant equipment and media segments, or if you link media segments together with equipment not described in the standard, then there is no way for the engineers to know how such equipment and media segments will behave. While such an Ethernet may function perfectly well, it will be "outside the standard," and you will not be able to use the configuration guidelines to verify that it meets the specifications for round trip timing, etc. Non-compliant equipment is described in more detail in Chapter 8.

7.3 Collision Domain

The multi-segment configuration guidelines apply only to a single Ethernet "collision domain." A collision domain is formally defined as a single CSMA/CD network in which there will be a collision if two computers attached to the system transmit at the same time.

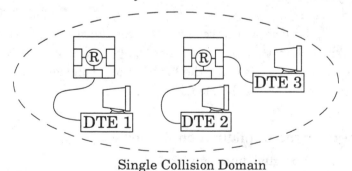

Single Collision Domain

FIGURE 7.1   Repeater hubs create a single collision domain

An Ethernet system composed of a single segment or multiple segments linked with repeaters is a network that functions as a single collision domain. The figure shows two repeater hubs connecting three computers. Since only repeater connections are used between segments in this network, all of the segments and computers are in the same collision domain.

In the next figure, the repeaters and DTEs are instead separated by a packet switch (switching hub, bridge, or router), and are therefore in separate collision domains, since packet switches do not forward collision signals from one segment to another. Packet switches contain multiple Ethernet interfaces and are designed to receive a packet on one Ethernet port and transmit the data onto another Ethernet port in a new packet.

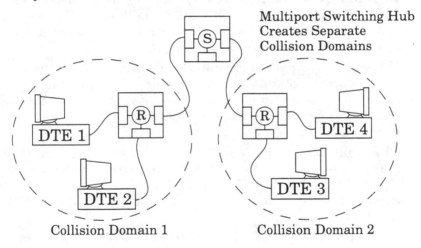

FIGURE 7.2   Switching hub creates separate collision domains

Instead of propagating collision signals between Ethernet segments, packet switches interrupt the collision domain and allow the Ethernets they link to operate independently. Therefore, you can use packet switching hubs to build larger network systems by interconnecting individual Ethernet systems.

The configuration guidelines described here are from the 802.3 standard, which describes the operation of a single Ethernet LAN. Therefore, the guidelines apply to a single collision domain only and have nothing to say about combining multiple Ethernets with packet switches. As long as each collision domain is configured properly it will function correctly, and you can link many such networks together using packet switching hubs.

7.4 10-Mbps Configuration Guidelines: Model 1

The first configuration model provides a set of multi-segment configuration rules for combining various 10-Mbps Ethernet segments. The bold text is taken directly from IEEE Std 802.3j-1993 (p.26). *[Italic text indicates my comments and is not from the standard.]*

1. **Repeater sets are required for all segment interconnection.** *[The repeaters used must comply with all IEEE specifications in section 9 of the 802.3 standard, and do signal retiming and reshaping, preamble regeneration, etc.]*

2. **MAUs that are part of repeater sets count toward the maximum number of MAUs on a segment.** *[Thick Ethernet repeaters typically use an outboard MAU to connect to the thick Ethernet coax. Thin coax and twisted-pair repeater hubs use internal MAUs located inside each repeater port.]*

3. **The transmission path permitted between any two DTEs may consist of up to five segments, four repeater sets (including optional AUIs), two MAUs, and two AUIs.** *[The repeater sets are assumed to have their own MAUs, which are not counted in this rule.]*

4. **AUI cables for 10BASE-FP and 10BASE-FL shall not exceed 25 m. (Since two MAUs per segment are required, 25 m per MAU results in a total AUI cable length of 50 m per segment).**

5. **When a transmission path consists of four repeaters and five segments, up to three of the segments may be mixing and the remainder must be link segments. When five segments are present, each fiber optic link segment (FOIRL, 10BASE-FB, or 10BASE-FL) shall not exceed 500 m, and each 10BASE-FP segment shall not exceed 300 m.**

6. **When a transmission path consists of three repeater sets and four segments, the following restrictions apply:**

   • **The maximum allowable length of any inter-repeater fiber segment shall not exceed 1000 m for FOIRL,**

10BASE-FB, and 10BASE-FL segments and shall not exceed 700 m for 10BASE-FP segments.

- **The maximum allowable length of any repeater to DTE fiber segment shall not exceed 400 m for 10BASE-FL segments and shall not exceed 300 m for 10BASE-FP segments and 400 m for segments terminated in a 10BASE-FL MAU.**

- **There is no restriction on the number of mixing segments in this case.** *[In other words, when using three repeater sets and four segments, all segments may be mixing segments if desired.]*

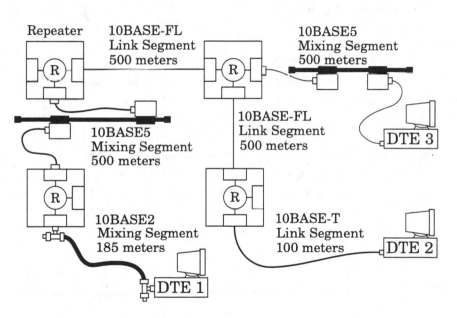

FIGURE 7.3   One possible maximum 10-Mbps configuration

The figure shows an example of a maximum Ethernet configuration that meets the canned configuration rules. The maximum packet transmission path in this system is between DTE 1 and DTE 2, since there are four repeaters and five media segments in that particular path. Two of the segments in the path are mixing segments, and the other three are link segments. You can find more examples in Appendix A, "10-Mbps Configuration Examples."

While the canned configuration rules are based on conservative timing calculations, you shouldn't let that lead you to believe that you can bend these rules and always get away with it. There isn't a lot of engineering margin left in maximum-sized Ethernets, despite the allowances made in the standards for manufacturing tolerances and equipment variances. If you want maximum performance and reliability, then you need to stick to the published guidelines.

Also, while the configuration guidelines emphasize the maximum limits of the system, you should beware of stretching things as far as they can go. Ethernets, like many other systems, work best when they are not being pushed to their limits.

7.5 10-Mbps Configuration Guidelines: Model 2

The second configuration model provided by the IEEE provides a set of calculation aids which make it possible for you to check the validity of more complex Ethernet systems. In the calculation model there are two sets of calculations that must be performed for each Ethernet system that you wish to evaluate. The first set of calculations verifies the round trip signal delay time. The second set of calculations verifies that the amount of interframe gap shrinkage is within the correct limits. Both calculations are based on network models that evaluate the worst-case path through the network.

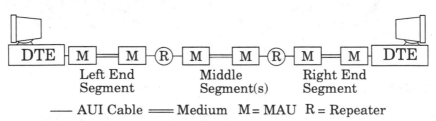

FIGURE 7.4   Network model for round trip timing

Figure 7.4 shows the network model used for calculating the round trip timing of the worst-case path. The model includes a left end segment, a right end segment, and as many middle segments as needed.To check the round trip timing on your network, you make a similar model of the worst-case path in your LAN. We will show how the round trip timing model is used by evaluating two sample networks later in this chapter. The network model used for interframe gap shrinkage is very similar to the round trip timing model, as you will see in the section on calculating interframe gap shrinkage.

Calculating Round Trip Delay Time

One goal of the configuration guidelines is to make sure that any two stations (DTEs) can contend fairly for access to the shared Ethernet channel if they happen to transmit at the same time. When this happens, each station attempting to transmit must be notified of channel contention (collision) by receiving a collision signal within the correct collision timing window.

The way to verify that your Ethernet system meets the limits is by calculating the total path delay (round trip timing) of the worst-case path in your system. This is done using "segment delay values" which are provided in bit times for each segment type. A bit time is the amount of time required to send one data bit on the network. Table 7.1 on the next page shows the segment delay values used to calculate the total worst-case path delay

To calculate the round trip delay value for each segment in your LAN, you multiply the length of the segment (in meters) times the delay factor listed in the last column of the table for the segment type, and add the result to the "Base" value for the segment in question. If the segment is at the maximum length, or if you're not sure of the segment length and want to use the maximum length in your calculations just to be safe, then instead of calculating the segment delay time you can simply use the "Max" value listed in the table for that segment.

Once you have calculated the segment delay values for each segment in the worst-case path on your LAN, you then add the segment delay values together to find the total path delay. To this total you add a margin of 5 bit times. **If the result is less than or equal to 575 bit times, the path passes the test**. The value of 575 bit times ensures that a DTE at the end of a worst-case path will not send more than

511 bits of the frame plus the 64 bits of frame preamble and SFD[1] (511 + 64 = 575) before the DTE is notified of the collision and stops transmitting.

TABLE 7.1 Round-trip delay values in bit times[a]

Segment Type	Max Len.	Left End Base	Left End Max	Mid-Segment Base	Mid-Segment Max	Right End Base	Right End Max	RT Delay/ meter
10BASE5	500	11.75	55.05	46.5	89.8	169.5	212.8	0.0866
10BASE2	185	11.75	30.731	46.5	65.48	169.5	188.48	0.1026
FOIRL	1000	7.75	107.75	29	129	152	252	0.1
10BASE-T	100[b]	15.25	26.55	42	53.3	165	176.3	0.113
10BASE-FP	1000	11.25	111.25	61	161	183.5	284	0.1
10BASE-FB	2000	N/A[c]	N/A	24	224	N/A	N/A	0.1
10BASE-FL	2000	12.25	212.25	33.5	233.5	156.5	356.5	0.1
Excess AUI	48	0	4.88	0	4.88	0	4.88	0.1026

a. Copyright © 1993 IEEE. All Rights Reserved.

b. Actual maximum segment length depends on cable characteristics.

c. N/A = Not Applicable: 10BASE-FB does not support end connections.

If the path you are checking has left and right end segments of different segment types, then you must check the path twice. The first time through you use one of the segment types as a left end segment, and the second time you use the other segment type as a left end segment. The path must pass the delay calculations in both directions. We will show how this is done in the complex sample network later in this chapter.

---

1. The frame preamble consists of seven bytes of an alternating pattern of ones and zeroes, followed by eight bits of the Start Frame Delimiter (SFD). The SFD contains a pattern of 10101011, which indicates to the Ethernet interface that the bits following this pattern are the start of the frame being sent.

Calculating the Interframe Gap Shrinkage

The interframe gap is a 96 bit time delay provided between frame transmissions to allow the network interfaces and other components some recovery time between frames. As a series of frames travel through a LAN the variable timing delays in network components, combined with the effects of signal reconstruction circuits in the repeaters, can result in a shrinkage of the interframe gap. Too small a gap between frames can overrun the frame reception rate of network interfaces, leading to lost frames. Therefore, it's important to ensure that a minimum interframe gap is maintained.

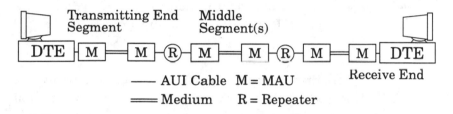

FIGURE 7.5   Network model for interframe gap shrinkage

The network model for checking the interframe gap shrinkage looks a lot like the round trip path delay model, except that it includes a "transmitting end" segment.

When doing the calculations for interframe gap shrinkage, only the transmitting end and the middle segments are of interest, since signals on these segments must travel through a repeater to reach the receiving end computer. The final segment connected to the receiving DTE does not contribute any gap shrinkage and is not included in the interframe gap calculations.

The following table provides the values used for calculating inter-frame gap shrinkage.

TABLE 7.2 Interframe gap shrinkage in bit times[a]

Segment Type	Transmitting End	Mid-segment
Coax	16	11
Link except 10BASE-FB	10.5	8
10BASE-FB	N/A[b]	2
10BASE-FP	11	8

a. Table Copyright © 1993. IEEE. All Rights Reserved.

b. N/A: Not Applicable: 10BASE-FB does not support end connections.

In a network where the receive and transmit end segments are not the same media type, you use the end segment with the largest number of shrinkage bit times as the "transmitting end" for the purposes of this calculation. This will provide the worst-case value for interframe gap shrinkage. **If the total is less than or equal to 49 bit times, the path passes the shrinkage test.**

Finding the Worst-Case Path

You begin the process of checking your network by finding the path in the network with the maximum delay. This is the path with the longest round trip time and largest number of repeaters between two stations (DTEs). In some cases you may decide that you have more than one candidate for worst-case path in your system. If that's the case, identify all the paths through your network that look like they are worst-case. Then do the calculations for each worst-case path you have found. If any path exceeds the limits for round trip timing or interframe gap, then the network system does not pass the test.

You should have a complete and up-to-date map of your network on hand that you can use to find the worst-case path between two DTEs. However, if your system is not well documented then you will have to investigate and map the network yourself. You need to find out what kinds of segments are in use, how long they are, the location of all repeaters, and how the system is laid out. Once you have this information, then you can determine what the maximum path is and what kinds of segments are used in the maximum path.

Once you've found your worst-case path(s), then the next thing you do is make a model of your path using the network model in Figure 7.4. You do this by assigning the segment at one end of your worst-case path to be a left end segment, which leaves a right end segment and possibly one or more middle segments. To help do this, you can draw a sketch of your worst-case path, noting the segment types and lengths. Then simply assign one of the end segments to be the left end, which leaves you with a right end segment. All other segments in the path become middle segments.

7.6 A Simple Model 2 Configuration Example

Let's look at how all this works with a simple example first. The figure shows a network with three 10BASE-FL segments connected to a fiber optic multiport repeater. Two of the segments are 2 km (2000 m) in length, and one is 1.5 km in length.

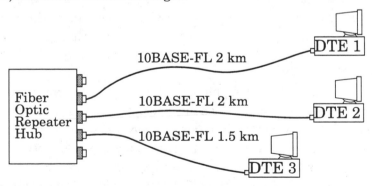

FIGURE 7.6   Simple configuration example

Even though this is a simple network, it is a configuration that is not described in the Model 1 canned configuration rules. Therefore, the only way to verify its operation is to perform the Model 2 calculations. By looking at the drawing, we see that the worst-case delay path is between DTE1 and DTE2, since this is the path with the longest distance between two DTEs. Next, let's evaluate this worst-case path for total round trip delay and interframe gap shrinkage.

Round Trip Delay

Since there are only two segments in the worst case path, our network model for round trip delay only has a left end and a right end segment. There are no middle segments to deal with. We'll assume for the purposes of this simple example that the fiber optic MAUs are connected directly to the DTEs and repeater, which eliminates the need to add extra bit times for AUI cable length. Both segments in the worst-case path are the maximum allowable length, which means we can simply use the Max values from the round-trip delay table.

According to Table 7.1, the Max left end segment delay value for a 2 km 10BASE-FL link is 212.25 bit times. For the 2 km right end segment the Max delay value is 356.5 bit times. Add them together, plus 5 bit times margin, and the total is: 573.75 bit times. This is less than the 575 maximum bit time budget that is allowed for a 10-Mbps network, which means that the worst-case path is OK. All shorter paths will have smaller delay values, so all paths in this Ethernet system meet the requirements of the standard as far as round trip timing is concerned. Next, let's look at the interframe gap shrinkage.

Interframe Gap Shrinkage

Since there are only two segments, we only have to look at a single transmitting end segment when calculating the interframe gap shrinkage. There are no middle segments to deal with, and the receive end segment does not count in the interframe gap calculations. Since both segments are the same segment type, finding the worst-case value is easy. According to Table 7.2, the interframe gap value for all link segments except 10BASE-FB is 10.5 bit times, and that becomes our total shrinkage value for this worst-case path. This is well under the 49 bit times of interframe shrinkage that is allowed for a 10-Mbps network.

As you can see, a network with a single repeater hop and whose worst-case delay path includes two maximum-length 10BASE-FL segments meets both the round trip delay requirements and the interframe shrinkage requirements, and is a valid network according to the Model 2 configuration method.

7.7 A Complex Model 2 Configuration Example

Next, let's look at a more complex example. In this example we're going to encounter lots of different segment types, extra AUI cables, etc. All these extra bits and pieces make the example much more complex to explain, although the basic process of looking up the bit times and adding them together is still quite simple. Nonetheless, be warned that for the next several pages I will be droning on and on about extra delay times for AUI cables, swapping left and right end segments, and so on.

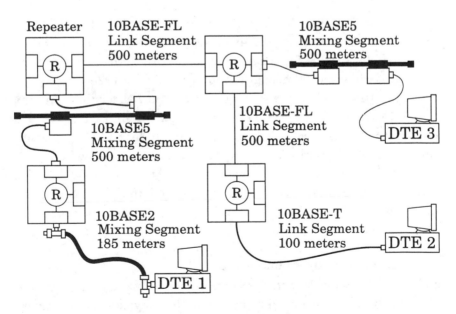

FIGURE 7.7   Complex configuration example

Figure 7.7 is a copy of the maximum length network shown earlier in this chapter. This figure shows one possible maximum-length system using four repeaters and five segments, and will be used here for the complex configuration example. As we've seen, the Model 1 rule-based configuration method shows that this network is OK. To check that, we'll evaluate this network using the calculation method provided in Model 2.

We start by finding the worst-case path in the sample network. By examination, you can see that the path in Figure 7.7 between DTE1 and DTE2 is the maximum delay path, since it contains the largest number of segments and repeaters in the path between any two DTEs in the network. Next, we make a network model out of the worst-case path. Let's start the process by assigning the thin Ethernet end segment to be the left end segment. That leaves us with three middle segments composed of a 10BASE5 segment and two fiber optic link segments, and a right end segment composed of a 10BASE-T link segment.

Next, we find out what the segment delay value is for a 10BASE2 left end segment. We could calculate the segment delay value by adding the left end base value for 10BASE2 coax (11.75) to the product of the round trip delay times the length in meters (185 * 0.1026 = 18.981) to come up with a total segment delay value of 30.731 for the thin coax segment. However, since 185 meters is the maximum segment length allowed for 10BASE2 segments, we can simply look up the Max left hand segment value in the table, which, not surprisingly, is 30.731. The 10BASE2 thin Ethernet segment is shown attached directly to the DTE and repeater, and there is no AUI cable in use. Therefore, we don't have to add any "excess AUI" cable length timing to the value for this segment.

Calculating Separate Left End Values

Since the left and right end segments in our worst-case path are different media types, we need to do the path delay calculations twice. We first calculate the total path delay using the 10BASE2 segment as the left end segment and the 10BASE-T segment as the right end. Then we swap their places and make the calculation again, using the 10BASE-T segment as the left end segment this time, and the

10BASE2 segment as the right end segment. The largest value that results from the two calculations is the one that we must use in verifying the network.

AUI Delay Value

The segment delay values provided in the table include allowances for an AUI cable of up to two meters length at each end of the segment (except for 10BASE-FB segments which connect directly to special repeater hubs and do not use AUI cables.) This takes care of any timing delays that may occur for AUI wires inside the ports of a repeater, for example.

On the other hand, media systems with external MAUs connected with AUI cables typically have AUI cables longer than two meters. To account for the timing delay in these AUI cables you can find out how long the AUI cables are, and use that length times the round trip delay per meter to develop an extra AUI cable delay time which is then added to the total path delay calculation. If you're not sure how long the AUI cables in your network are, you can use the maximum delay shown for an AUI cable, which is 4.88 for all segment locations, left end, middle, or right end.

Calculating Middle Segment Values

Let's continue the process of finding the total round trip delay time by doing the calculations for the middle segments. In the worst-case path for the network in Figure 7.7 there are three middle segments composed of a maximum length 10BASE5 segment, and two 500 meter long 10BASE-FL fiber optic segments. By looking in the table under mid-segments we find that the 10BASE5 segment has a Max delay value of 89.8.

Note that the repeaters are connected to the 10BASE5 with AUI cables and outboard MAUs. That means we need to add the delay for two AUI cables. Let's assume that we don't know how long the AUI cables are, therefore we'll use the value for two maximum-length AUI cables in the segment, one at each connection to a repeater. That gives us an AUI cable delay of 9.76 to add to the total path delay.

We can calculate the segment delay value for the 10BASE-FL mid-segments by multiplying the 500 meter length of each segment times the RT Delay/meter, which is 0.1, which gives us a result of 50. We then add 50 to the mid-segment base value for a 10BASE-FL segment, which is 33.5, for a total segment delay of 83.5.

Even though it's not shown in Figure 7.7, fiber optic links often use outboard fiber optic MAUs and AUI cables. Just to make things a little harder, let's assume that we used two AUI cables of 25 meters each to make a connection from the repeaters to outboard fiber optic MAUs on the 10BASE-FL segments. That gives us a total of 50 meters of AUI cable on each 10BASE-FL segment. Since we have two such middle segments we can represent the total AUI cable length for both segments by adding 9.76 extra bit times to the total path delay.

Completing the Round Trip Timing Calculation

Given that we started our calculations with the 10BASE-2 segment assigned to the left end segment, that leaves us with a right end segment of 10BASE-T twisted-pair Ethernet. This segment is 100 meters long, which is the length provided in the "Max" column for a 10BASE-T segment. Depending on the cable quality, a 10BASE-T segment can be longer than 100 meters, but we'll assume that the link in our example is 100 meters. That makes the Max value for the 10BASE-T right end segment 176.3. Adding all the segment delay values together we get the following:

TABLE 7.3 Round trip path delay with 10BASE2 left end segment

Left End	10BASE2	30.731
Mid-segment	10BASE5	89.8
Mid-segment	10BASE-FL	83.5
Mid-segment	10BASE-FL	83.5
Right End	10BASE-T	176.3
Excess Length AUI	Quan. Four	19.52
	Path Delay =	483.351

To complete the process, we need to perform a second set of calculations with the left and right segments swapped. In this case, the left end becomes a maximum length 10BASE-T segment, with a value of 26.55, and the right end becomes a maximum length 10BASE-2 segment with a value of 188.48. Adding the bit time values again, we get the following:

TABLE 7.4 Round trip path delay with 10BASE-T left end segment

Left End	10BASE-T	26.55
Mid-segment	10BASE5	89.8
Mid-segment	10BASE-FL	83.5
Mid-segment	10BASE-FL	83.5
Right End	10BASE2	188.48
Excess Length AUI	Quan. Three	19.52
	Path Delay =	491.35

Since the second set of calculations produced a larger value, this is the value we must use for the worst-case round trip delay for this Ethernet. Finally, the standard recommends adding a margin of five bit times to form the total path delay value. We are allowed to add anywhere from zero to five bits margin, but five bit times is recommended.

Adding five bit times for margin brings us up to a total delay value of 496.35 bit times, which is less than the maximum of 575 bit times that is allowed. Therefore, our complex sample network is qualified in terms of the worst-case round trip timing delay. All shorter paths will have smaller delay values, so all paths in the Ethernet system shown in Figure 7.7 meet the requirements of the standard as far as round trip timing is concerned.

Interframe Gap Shrinkage

We finish the evaluation of the network shown in Figure 7.7 by calculating the worst-case interframe gap shrinkage for that network. This is done by evaluating the same worst-case path that we used in the path delay calculations. However, for the purposes of calculating gap shrinkage we only evaluate the transmitting and mid-segments.

Once again we start by applying the network model to the worst-case path. For interframe gap shrinkage the transmitting segment should be assigned the end segment in the worst-case path that has the largest shrinkage value. As shown in Table 7.2, the coax segment has the largest value, so we will assign the 10BASE2 segment to the role of transmitting end segment. The mid segments consist of one coax and two link segments. That leaves the 10BASE-T receive end segment which is simply ignored. The totals are:

TABLE 7.5 Total interframe gap shrinkage

Transmitting End Coax	16
Mid-segment Coax	11
Mid-segment Link	8
Mid-segment Link	8
Total PVV =	43

As you can see, the total path variability value for our sample network equals 43. This is less than the 49 bit time maximum allowed in the standard, which means that this network meets the requirements for interframe gap shrinkage.

CHAPTER 8   Miscellaneous Issues for 10-Mbps Networks

8.1 Miscellaneous Issues

This chapter describes several issues that you may encounter when configuring and using 10-Mbps network segments. This includes the use of the AUI connector to provide a universal connection to any segment. Also included is a description of how stackable repeaters work. Following that, we look at the issue of compliance with the Ethernet standard, and how some equipment sold today may not be fully compliant. Finally, the SQE Test signal provided on external MAUs is explained, including how to correctly configure an external MAU for SQE Test.

8.2 The Universal AUI Connector

The 15-pin AUI connector on an Ethernet interface provides a universal connector that makes it possible to attach an Ethernet interface to any 10-Mbps segment type with an external MAU.

The chapter on 10BASE5 thick Ethernet shows how an AUI-equipped interface is attached to a thick Ethernet segment. This is the original Ethernet connection scheme, and it is the only way an Ethernet interface can be attached to a thick coaxial cable.

Direct Media Connections

As other media systems based on lighter weight cables were developed, it became possible to attach the newer media segments directly to the interface using an appropriate connector. That's how the 10BASE2 thin coax and 10BASE-T twisted-pair systems work. The drawback to this scheme is that it can limit your connection options to a single media type. If the Ethernet interface in your computer is equipped only with a 10BASE2 BNC connector, for example, then it can only connect to a 10BASE2 segment. If your office is equipped only with a 10BASE-T twisted-pair segment, then you have a problem.

The standard notes that separate segments must be linked with a repeater. To make this connection in a manner that complies with the standard, you need to buy a repeater with both 10BASE2 and 10BASE-T ports on it. Then you can use a short 10BASE2 segment to connect the computer to one port of the repeater, and the other port of the repeater is connected to the 10BASE-T segment. Obviously this is more complex and expensive than we'd prefer. Given the widespread popularity of the 10BASE-T system, you will also find vendors selling Ethernet cards with only 10BASE-T 8-pin jacks on them.

Rather than limit your options in this way, many vendors sell Ethernet cards with all three commonly used segment connectors on them: a 15-pin AUI connector, a 10BASE2 BNC connector, and a 10BASE-T RJ-45 connector. Another approach is for the vendor to provide only a 15-pin AUI connector on the interface, since that is the universal interface to all MAUs, providing a connection to any 10-Mbps media system.

AUI Connections to All 10-Mbps Media Types
The chapter on 10BASE5 thick coax illustrates an external MAU connection using an AUI cable. In the chapter on the fiber optic media system, we saw an AUI connection to an external 10BASE-FL fiber optic MAU (FOMAU). This is a typical connection scheme for fiber optic segments.

You can also make a connection to a thin Ethernet segment by using an external thin Ethernet MAU. The MAU with its BNC connector is attached directly to a BNC Tee on the thin Ethernet coax. The 15-pin AUI connector on the MAU is connected to the 15-pin AUI connector on the Ethernet interface, either with an AUI cable or directly. You can connect the MAU directly to the 15-pin AUI connector on the Ethernet interface if the MAU is small enough to fit. This eliminates the need for an AUI cable.

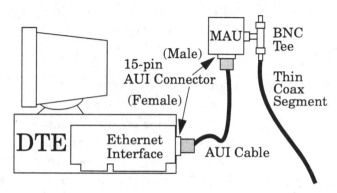

FIGURE 8.1   AUI-equipped interface attached to a 10BASE2 segment

In much the same way, you can make a connection from an Ethernet interface equipped with a 15-pin AUI to a twisted-pair Ethernet segment. The other end of the twisted-pair segment is typically connected to a twisted-pair hub. Once again, you can attach the MAU to the interface with an AUI cable, or dispense with the AUI cable if the MAU is small enough to fit directly onto the 15-pin AUI connector.

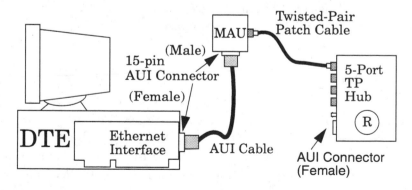

FIGURE 8.2   AUI-equipped interface attached to a 10BASE-T segment

Note that the hub (repeater) is equipped with its own female AUI port, like the one found on a DTE. This allows the hub to be connected to a media segment by way of an external MAU. Therefore, you cannot make a direct connection between the AUI port on a DTE and the AUI port on a hub. AUI ports are designed to be connected to a network segment with an external MAU, and they will not function correctly if directly connected to one another.

Not All AUI Connectors Are The Same

The vast majority of vendors in the Ethernet marketplace use a standard 15-pin "D-Type"[1] AUI connector on their Ethernet equipment, but you need to be aware that there are a few exceptions. Occasionally a vendor will supply an AUI connector that does not use the 15-pin connector described in the IEEE standard, but instead uses a vendor-specific connector. This is sometimes done to conserve space on an Ethernet interface, or to ensure that the customer uses a specific kind of MAU provided by the vendor.

The Apple AUI (AAUI) connector is an example of this approach. The AAUI connector supplied on Apple computers with built-in Ethernet interfaces is not a standard 15-pin "D" type connector. To connect this type of computer to an Ethernet segment you need to buy a MAU equipped with a built-in Apple AUI cable that has the Apple-specific connector on one end. The Apple 10BASE5 MAU with AAUI connector comes with an external power supply, which provides a source of +12 volt power for the MAU.

The IEEE 802.3 standard recommends the use of the 15-pin D-Type AUI connector to ensure interoperability with other vendors, but the standard does not require the use of that connector. Therefore, a company such as Apple can equip their computers with a different kind of AUI connector. That way they can be sure that their customers will buy MAUs that are specially designed to work with Apple equipment.

---

1. So named because the shape of the connector end is roughly that of the letter "D."

You may also see other vendors use the Apple AUI connector on their laptop computers, since it is smaller than the 15-pin D-type AUI connector, and the use of an externally powered 10BASE5 MAU solves the problem of providing power from the laptop for that type of MAU.

8.3 Stackable Repeaters

The original Ethernet repeater was a simple device that was designed to connect two segments together. You can still buy two-port repeaters, but now there are also multiport repeaters (hubs) available that support connections to all manner of Ethernet media types in a single box. Vendors have also made it possible to link some kinds of repeater hubs together so that they can function as one large repeater. Repeaters that support this special connection are generally known as "stackable" repeaters.

Operation of Stackable Repeaters

Stackable repeaters are designed to allow you to connect individual repeater hubs together so that the ports on the combined devices operate as a single large repeater. This allows you to link ports on separate repeaters so that they function together as a single "repeater hop."

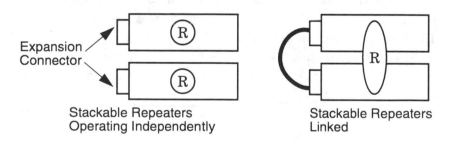

Stackable Repeaters
Operating Independently

Stackable Repeaters
Linked

FIGURE 8.3   Stackable repeaters

In the figure two stackable repeaters are shown operating independently and linked. When operating independently, the special expansion connector is not used, and each repeater counts as a single repeater hop in the configuration guidelines.

When the special expansion connector is used to link stackable repeaters together, the ports on both repeaters are combined. The expansion connector links the internal repeater electronics of each box, so that the combined set of repeater ports now function as a single repeater. Stackable repeaters make it possible for you to add repeater devices at a given point in your network and link them together so that they function as a single logical repeater as far as the configuration guidelines are concerned.

Each vendor uses a different scheme for the expansion cable and connection system, so you typically cannot link stackable repeaters from different vendors. Further, the expansion cable is short, usually only a foot or so in length. This means that stackable repeaters must be close together, preferably stacked directly on top of one another as the name implies. Finally, since the design of a stackable repeater and expansion bus is different for each vendor, you need to pay careful attention to each vendor's guidelines and instructions on how to link their stackable repeater together, and how many repeaters and ports may be linked.

Be aware that some vendors label their repeaters "stackable," but only mean that their repeaters can be piled on top of one another and linked with an external Ethernet segment. This is the original method of linking repeaters on Ethernet, but it does not provide the special advantage of combining the ports in two or more repeaters so that they function as a single repeater. If in doubt, ask the vendor whether all repeater ports on the separate devices can be linked so as to function as a single repeater hop.

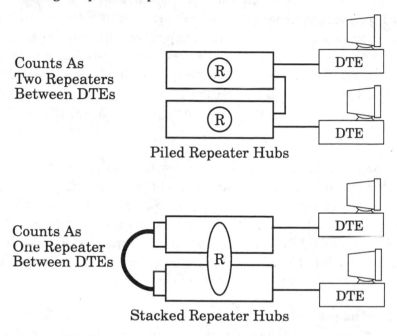

FIGURE 8.4   Counting repeater hops between DTEs

The figure shows two configurations using repeaters. In the first configuration, two DTEs are linked with two separate repeaters. The two separate repeaters are linked together with a standard Ethernet segment of some kind (thin Ethernet, twisted-pair Ethernet, etc.) This configuration counts as two repeaters in the path between the two DTEs.

In the second configuration, two DTEs are linked together using repeater ports on two stackable repeaters. The stackable repeaters have been connected together using the special expansion port, and all ports are functioning as a single repeater. This configuration counts as one repeater in the signal path between the two DTEs.

8.4 Levels of Compliance with the Standard

Stackable repeaters are an example of an innovation that uses standard components (repeater chips) and provides more flexible ways to hook them up while maintaining compliance with the signal timing and media specs in the standard. Devices like stackable repeaters that provide clever extensions to the set of Ethernet equipment are designed to be used without causing any problems in the signal timing of any Ethernet system from the smallest to the largest allowed in the guidelines.

On the other hand, there are some devices and components on the market that do not fully comply with the specifications. These devices may work well for a small network, but could cause problems with signal timing in a large net. When such devices are not fully compliant with the standard equipment and media specifications, they cannot be evaluated using the IEEE configuration guidelines. Some examples of these devices are described later in this chapter.

In developing a technical standard, the IEEE is careful to include only those items whose behavior must be carefully specified to make the system work. Therefore, all Ethernet interfaces must comply fully with the MAC specifications so as to perform the medium access control functions identically. Otherwise the network may not function correctly. At the same time, the IEEE makes an effort not to constrain the market by standardizing such things as the appearance of an Ethernet interface, or how many connectors it should have on it. The intent is to provide just enough engineering specifications to make the system work reliably, without inhibiting competition and the inventiveness of the marketplace.

In general the IEEE has been quite successful. However, the inventiveness of the marketplace sometimes leads to the development of devices that are not fully compliant with the timing specs or media specs in the standard. These devices include AUI port concentrators, media stretchers, media converters, etc.

The Effect of Standards Compliance

How much you should be concerned about all this is largely up to you and your particular circumstances. Another way of saying this is: "Optimality differs according to context."[2] It's up to you to decide how important these issues are, given your particular circumstances (or "context").

For one thing, not all network innovations are a bad idea. After all, thin coaxial Ethernet and twisted-pair Ethernet started life as vendor innovations that later became carefully specified media systems in the IEEE standard. On the other hand, if you want your network to operate as predictably and stably as possible given a variety of vendor equipment and traffic loads, then one way to help achieve that goal is by using only equipment that complies with all IEEE specifications, and by following the official configuration guidelines.

If you are building an Ethernet that just connects a couple of computers in your house, for example, you may feel that any special equipment you can find that helps make this type of setup happen at the least cost is a good deal. If the equipment isn't 100% compliant with every detail of the standard, you may not care all that much. Given that you are probably building a small network system, and given that you probably don't intend for the network to grow very large, then you may decide that you are not all that worried about multi-vendor interoperability or about your ability to evaluate the network using the IEEE configuration guidelines.

However, if you are a network manager of a departmental or campus network system, then people will be depending on that network to get their work done, which changes your context quite a bit. Departmental nets are always growing, so now it's the case that extending networks to accommodate growth is a major priority for you. Also,

2. I am indebted to M. A. Padlipsky for this useful advice, which was published in a "bridge vs. routers" debate in <u>IEEE Network</u>, Vol.2 No.1, January 1988, p.93

network stability under all sorts of traffic loads becomes another important issue for you. In this context, multi-vendor interoperability and compliance with the IEEE configuration guidelines becomes much more important. You can help achieve this by making sure that the equipment you use meets the IEEE specifications, and making sure that you follow the official configuration guidelines.

Which Equipment is Not Fully Compliant?

While the vast majority of Ethernet equipment sold is fully compliant with the standard, there's no LAN industry organization that will certify and stamp equipment "100% Compliant with all Applicable IEEE Specifications." Therefore, you need to be wary about believing everything you read in equipment catalogs. Sometimes it seems like vendors use the term "compliant" to simply mean "can successfully send Ethernet signals to other equipment." They may not tell you whether the component they are selling exactly conforms to all applicable IEEE specifications, and whether it is a piece of standard and interoperable equipment that is widely available from other vendors and that is covered under the IEEE configuration guidelines.

Let's look next at some of the most commonly used items that either are not described in the standards or that may not be fully compliant with the standards.

AUI Port Concentrator (DELNI)

The AUI port concentrator unit is also called a port multiplier, transceiver multiplexor, or fan-out unit. The original port concentrator was developed by DEC and called the DELNI (for "Digital Ethernet Local Network Interconnect"). Port concentrators sold by other vendors are sometimes referred to as DELNIs or called "DELNI-like" devices. The port concentrator was developed when thick Ethernet was the only media type available, and network designers faced a problem when it came to connecting a set of machines clustered together in a small space.

The problem arises because the thick Ethernet standard requires that each MAU attachment be separated by at least 2.5 meters of cable from the next MAU attachment. This meant that when you needed to connect a number of machines located near one another to the network, you had to coil up enough thick Ethernet coax in a wiring closet or under a machine room floor to provide sufficient cable to meet the 2.5 meter MAU spacing requirement.

By providing several (usually eight) AUI ports in a single device, vendors made it easier to connect groups of computers to thick Ethernet. The eight computers are attached to the male AUI connectors on the port concentrator. The concentrator has its own female AUI "network" port which provides a way to connect the concentrator to a network segment using an external MAU. In effect, all eight computers end up sharing the single external MAU connection to the network segment. The eight computers are not penalized for sharing a single MAU, since only one computer can transmit on an Ethernet at any given time.

In terms of the timing delay budget for a standard Ethernet, the concentrator unit sits in the AUI cable path between the Ethernet segment and the DTE. The added signal delay and other effects contributed by the electronics inside the concentrator are not accounted for in the IEEE standard. These effects on the signal may vary depending upon which vendor built the concentrator. Also, since the concentrator is not described in the standard, a network system using concentrators cannot be verified using the IEEE configuration guidelines.

If you use port concentrators you should read the vendor's configuration guidelines and follow them carefully. Even then you may find that the signal delays and other effects contributed by concentrators may cause problems in very large networks, or when stations are attached to the concentrator with long AUI cables.

Media Converters

The IEEE configuration guidelines state that repeaters must be used to link all segment types. It used to be the case that repeaters were fairly expensive, and could add a significant cost to a network design. Therefore, some vendors attempted to deal with this by offering a lower cost device called a media converter. These devices are also called media adapters and media translators, depending on the vendor.

Media converters are designed to link media segments together inexpensively without using a full-fledged repeater. While they provide some of the signal amplification functions of a repeater, they do not contain the more expensive circuits used by a repeater to retime signals, rebuild the preamble on the Ethernet frame, partition (isolate) the segment in case of errors, and so on. The lack of these more expensive circuits explains why media converters were a lower-cost approach to linking segments than repeaters. However, the cost differential between media converters and true 802.3 repeaters has been dropping ever since low-cost repeater chips became more widely available due to the popularity of the twisted-pair Ethernet system.

An Ethernet system that includes media converters cannot be evaluated using the IEEE configuration guidelines, since the media converter is not part of the standard set of equipment defined in the Ethernet specifications. To make sure that you can evaluate your network using the official configuration rules, you need to use IEEE 802.3 repeaters for all segment interconnections. If in doubt when buying a device that links segments together, ask the vendor to verify that what they are selling is a true IEEE 802.3 repeater, and that it meets all of the specifications in section 9 of the 802.3 standard.

Special Media Segments

Another area of vendor innovation is the media segment. You can find products on the market that make it possible to use twisted-pair Ethernet in a daisy chain topology instead of the point-to-point topology described in the 10BASE-T specifications and covered under the configuration guidelines. There are also devices that extend the reach of a twisted-pair segment considerably beyond what is described in the specifications.

Any or all of these devices may work just fine for you as long as you are aware of their limitations. In most cases these are proprietary devices that can only be purchased from a single vendor, or just a few vendors. They also come with their own vendor-specific configuration guidelines, since they are not described in the IEEE standard. It's up to you to evaluate such devices with respect to your needs and network circumstances.

8.5 The SQE Test Signal for External MAUs

When you install an external MAU on your Ethernet system it is extremely important to correctly configure the SQE Test signal. SQE Test is a signal that must be disabled if the MAU is attached to a repeater (hub). For all other devices that may be attached to an external MAU, the standard recommends that the SQE Test signal be enabled.

The purpose of this signal is to test the important collision detection electronics of the MAU, and to let the Ethernet interface know that the collision detection circuits and signal paths are working correctly. The earliest Ethernet standard, DIX V1.0 published in 1980, did not include a test signal for the collision detection system. However, in the DIX V2.0 specifications published in 1982, the MAU was provided with a new signal called Collision Presence Test (CPT) whose nickname was "heartbeat." The name was changed to SQE Test in the 1985 IEEE 802.3 standard.

Operation of SQE Test

The way the SQE Test, or heartbeat, signal works is simple: after every frame is sent, the MAU waits a few bit times and then sends a short burst (about 10 bit times) of the collision presence signal over the collision signal wires of the AUI cable back to the Ethernet interface, thereby testing the collision detection electronics and signal paths.

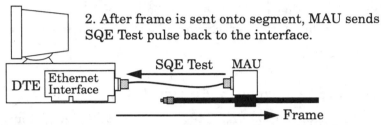

2. After frame is sent onto segment, MAU sends
SQE Test pulse back to the interface.

1. Ethernet interface sends frame through
MAU onto segment.

FIGURE 8.5   Normal SQE Test operation

The result is that the Ethernet interface in the computer receives an SQE Test signal on the collision signal wires of the AUI cable after every frame transmission made by the interface.

There are two things about SQE Test that it's important to understand:

1. The SQE Test signal is never sent out onto the network medium. SQE Test is only sent between the MAU and the Ethernet interface.

2. The SQE Test signal does not delay frame transmissions. Since the SQE Test pulse occurs during the interframe gap, no time is lost due to SQE Test signals. An Ethernet interface can send frames as fast as possible while also receiving SQE Test signals between every frame transmission.

The Changing Names of CPT and SQE Test

When the heartbeat signal was introduced in the early 1980s MAUs could be purchased without heartbeat, or with switch-selectable heartbeat so that you could turn it off. Today's MAUs all have a jumper or a switch that allows the heartbeat signal to be disabled. Only these days the signal is called SQE Test. SQE by itself is the name for the actual collision detection signal as distinct from the collision test signal. SQE stands for "Signal Quality Error," which is what the Collision Presence signal changed into in the IEEE 802.3 specifications.

Just to confuse things further you may find that some vendors do not label things correctly. For example, you may find that the switch for enabling the SQE Test signal will be labelled "SQE" instead of the correct "SQE Test." Since "SQE" is the name of the real collision signal, the last thing you'd want to do is disable the very important collision detection signal in Ethernet. Nonetheless, this confusion of terms is very widespread.

Repeaters and SQE Test

Given that SQE Test is an optional signal on an external MAU, when should SQE Test be enabled? The 802.3 standard recommends that SQE Test be enabled, with one major exception: **SQE Test must be shut off if the MAU is connected to an IEEE 802.3 repeater**. Note that the very commonly used twisted-pair Ethernet hub is a repeater. The reason for disabling SQE Test for 802.3 repeaters has to do with the timing of signals through a repeater.

To make all repeated segments function like one big segment (which is the repeater's role in life) it's important for a repeater to react to events on the network segments as fast as possible. Due to the interframe gap, a normal Ethernet interface in a computer has no need to react to anything immediately after a frame has been sent. A repeater, on the other hand, is required to monitor the signals on a network segment at all times, and does not have any "dead time" during which it can receive a SQE Test signal.

If you leave the SQE Test signal enabled on an external MAU that is connected to a repeater your network will probably continue to function, but you can end up with some signal interactions that may result in slower network performance. It is not unusual to see this problem, since it's pretty easy for an unsuspecting user or network manager to connect a repeater hub to an existing transceiver cable without looking into whether or not the MAU that the transceiver cable is connected to has SQE Test enabled. To see why you really don't want to do this, let's look next at what happens when a repeater receives SQE Test signals.

Misconfigured SQE Test and Slow Network Performance

It's possible to experience very slow network performance when SQE Test is mistakenly left on for a repeater connection. This can happen because of the interaction between a repeater and the SQE Test signal. Tests in the network lab show that if you leave the SQE Test signal enabled on an external MAU connected to a twisted-pair hub, for example, the repeater electronics in the hub mis-interpret each burst of SQE Test signal as news of a real collision.

With SQE Test enabled, the repeater sees what it thinks is a collision signal after every frame it transmits. The repeater regards this signal as a "receive collision," which is a collision that the repeater detects on the segment when the repeater itself is not actively transmitting a frame. Since one of the tasks of a repeater is to make sure all segments hear all collisions, the repeater sends a "collision enforcement jam" signal of 96 bits out onto all other ports of the repeater for each receive collision it thinks it hears.

This type of jam signal is part of the normal operation of the repeater. Sending a short burst of the collision enforcement jam signal onto the network segments upon detection of a receive collision is the way a repeater makes sure that all stations attached to network segments get news of the collision. However, the more frames sent through a repeater connected to a MAU with SQE Test incorrectly enabled, the more jam signals are generated. A flood of falsely generated jam signals occupies time on the network, even though they will not be seen by most monitoring devices. That's because most monitoring devices count full-sized frames as traffic and cannot detect very short events like a jam sequence.

A network has a given amount of idle time available for frame transmission, depending on the traffic rate, transmitted frame sizes, etc. A flood of unnecessary jam sequences can cause idle time starvation, which in turn makes it more difficult for the computers attached to the network to transmit a frame. The result is that users may report a "slow network." And since the jam fragments are not visible to network monitoring devices, the monitors might report a reasonable traffic rate while the network is acting as though it is heavily loaded. That's why you want to be absolutely certain that the SQE Test signal is turned off when attaching a repeater to a MAU on your network.

Note that despite the use of an incorrectly configured external MAU, the network will continue to function more or less adequately, although higher traffic rates will generate more and more jams, leading to slower and slower network response. If two or more MAUs are misconfigured, it's possible to get into a self-sustaining loop and generate so many jam sequences that the network effectively comes to a halt.

This whole issue of whether to enable or disable SQE Test affects only external MAUs. Repeaters with built-in thin Ethernet and twisted-pair Ethernet MAUs have their MAU chips wired up with the SQE Test signal disabled. It's only external MAUs attached to 15-pin AUI connectors that can be configured incorrectly for a repeater.

Computers and SQE Test

For computers (DTEs) attached to a network segment with external MAUs, the standard recommends that SQE Test be enabled. That's because the absence of an SQE Test signal after a frame transmission can alert the Ethernet interface that there may be a problem with the collision detection circuits. The failure of the SQE Test signal to show up after a transmission could be an indication that something may be wrong with the collision detect circuit, or the signal path between the MAU and interface. It could be caused by something simple, like an AUI cable having come loose. Or it could be a more serious problem, like the collision detection circuits in the MAU having failed.

Without a correctly functioning collision detect system, the Ethernet interface in your computer could end up ignoring collisions on the network and transmitting at incorrect times. While rare, this kind of failure can be quite difficult to debug. Therefore, you would like there to be some way for the software on your station to let you know if it detects a problem through the absence of an SQE Test signal after a frame transmission.

However, even if the software on your station does detect the failure of the SQE Test signal to arrive after a frame transmission, it will typically just log the failure in a count of network interface errors maintained somewhere in computer memory by the interface software. These statistics are often not available to users without special programs designed to interrogate low-level software counters.

Most interface software is designed not to make a fuss if the SQE Test signal is missing because SQE Test is an optional signal on external MAUs and is not well understood by most users. Rather than take worried phone calls from people asking what the error message about SQE Test might mean, and rather than try and diagnose whether it's a real problem or just reflects the fact that the signal was intentionally disabled, many vendors take the approach of silently logging the presence or absence of SQE Test in a software counter somewhere.

Other Problems When Using SQE Test

One side effect of enabling SQE Test for all normal computers is that the SQE Test signal can cause the collision presence light to flash on some MAUs and interfaces equipped with troubleshooting lights. This can happen because the SQE Test pulse is sent over the same collision presence pair of wires in the AUI cable as a real collision signal, causing the troubleshooting light to flash for both real collisions and SQE Test signals. Therefore, if you enable SQE Test as recommended by the standard for all normal computers, you may need to ignore the effect that the SQE Test signal has on any collision presence lights on your network hardware.

By the way, the usual activity lights found on Ethernet equipment are only there to provide a rough indication of network activity. The duration of each flash of light must be artificially lengthened to make them visible to the human eye. For that reason, the lights can appear to be glowing steadily and may seem to indicate an overloaded network, when in reality the traffic and collision rates are those of a typically busy network with no severe problems.

SQE Test and AUI Port Concentrators

Something else to watch out for is the behavior of AUI port concentrators like the DELNI when they are attached to an external MAU with the SQE Test signal enabled. These concentrators will typically pass the SQE Test signal from the external MAU onto all ports of the concentrator, which can lead to problems if a repeater is connected to one of those ports.

CHAPTER 9   100-Mbps Media Systems, 100BASE-T Fast Ethernet

9.1 Which Fast Ethernet?

This guide describes the 802.3 Ethernet system, and the 100BASE-T Fast Ethernet segments which are part of that system. However, you should know that there are two LAN standards that can carry Ethernet frames at 100-Mbps.

When the IEEE standardization committee met to begin work on a faster Ethernet system, two approaches were presented. One approach was to speed up the original Ethernet system to 100-Mbps, keeping the original CSMA/CD medium access control mechanism. This approach is called 100BASE-T Fast Ethernet.

Another approach presented to the committee was to create an entirely new medium access control mechanism, one based on hubs that controlled access to the medium using a "demand priority" mechanism. This new access control system transports standard Ethernet frames, but it does it with a new medium access control mechanism. This system was further extended to allow it to transport token ring frames as well. As a result, this approach is now called 100VG-AnyLAN.

The IEEE decided to create standards for both approaches. The 100BASE-T Fast Ethernet standard described here is part of the original 802.3 standard. The 100VG-AnyLAN system is standardized under a new number: IEEE 802.12.

9.2 100-Mbps Media Systems

Compared to the 10-Mbps specifications, the 100-Mbps system results in a factor of ten reduction in the bit-time, which is the amount of time it takes to transmit a bit on the Ethernet channel. This produces a tenfold increase in the speed of the packets over the media system. However, the other important aspects of the Ethernet system including the frame format, the amount of data a frame may carry, and the media access control mechanism, are all unchanged.

The Fast Ethernet specifications include mechanisms for Auto-Negotiation of the media speed. This makes it possible for vendors to provide dual-speed Ethernet interfaces that can be installed and run at either 10-Mbps or 100-Mbps automatically.

There are three media varieties that have been specified for transmitting 100-Mbps Ethernet signals.

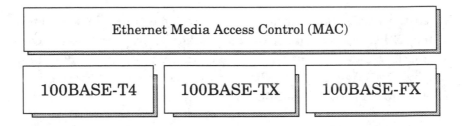

FIGURE 9.1   The three 100-Mbps Ethernet media varieties

The three media types are shown with their IEEE shorthand identifiers. The IEEE identifiers include three pieces of information. The first item, "100", stands for the media speed of 100-Mbps. The "BASE" stands for "baseband," which is a type of signaling. Baseband signaling simply means that Ethernet signals are the only signals carried over the media system.

The third part of the identifier provides an indication of the segment type. The "T4" segment type is a twisted-pair segment that uses four pairs of telephone-grade twisted-pair wire. The "TX" segment type is a twisted-pair segment that uses two pairs of wires and is based on the data grade twisted-pair physical medium standard developed by ANSI. The "FX" segment type is a fiber optic link segment based on the fiber optic physical medium standard developed by ANSI and that uses two strands of fiber cable. The TX and FX medium standards are collectively known as 100BASE-X.

The 100BASE-TX and 100BASE-FX media standards used in Fast Ethernet are both adopted from physical media standards first developed by ANSI, the American National Standards Institute. The ANSI physical media standards were originally developed for the Fiber Distributed Data Interface (FDDI) LAN standard (ANSI standard X3T9.5), and are widely used in FDDI LANs.

Rather than "re-inventing the wheel" when it came to signalling at 100-Mbps, the Fast Ethernet standard adapted these two ANSI media standards for use in the new Fast Ethernet medium specifications. The T4 standard was also provided to make it possible to use lower-quality twisted-pair wire for 100-Mbps Ethernet signals.

9.3 Components Used For a 100-Mbps Connection

Shown next is a block diagram of the components that can be used to make a connection to the 100-Mbps media system.

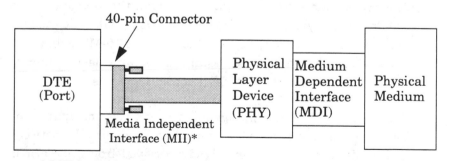

FIGURE 9.2   Block diagram of a 100-Mbps network connection

The figure shows the components defined in the IEEE standard for making an attachment to a 100-Mbps media system. These components differ somewhat from the ones used in a 10-Mbps system.

Physical Medium

Starting with the right hand side of the block diagram in the figure, we find the physical medium used to carry Ethernet signals between computers. This could be any one of the three 100-Mbps media types. You make a connection to the medium with the medium dependent interface, or MDI. This is an 8-pin twisted-pair connector or fiber optic connector in the 100BASE-T system.

Physical Layer Device

The next device in the block diagram is called the Physical Layer Device (PHY). This device performs the same general function as a transceiver in the 10-Mbps Ethernet system. It may be a set of integrated circuits inside the Ethernet port of a network device, therefore invisible to the user, or it may be a small box equipped with an MII cable, like the outboard transceiver and transceiver cable used in 10-Mbps Ethernet.

Medium Independent Interface

The MII is an optional set of electronics that provides a way to link the Ethernet medium access control functions in the network device with the Physical Layer Device (PHY) that sends signals onto the network medium. An MII may optionally support both 10-Mbps and 100-Mbps operation, allowing suitably equipped network devices to connect to both 10BASE-T and 100BASE-T media segments.

The MII is designed to make the signalling differences among the various media segments transparent to the Ethernet chips in the network device. The MII converts the line signals received from the various media segments by the transceiver (PHY) into digital format signals that are then provided to the Ethernet chips in the device. The optional MII electronics, and associated 40-pin female connector and MII cable, makes it possible to connect a network device to any of several media types, providing maximum flexibility.

The MII electronics may be linked to an outboard transceiver through a 40-pin MII connector and a short MII cable. The MII cable for use with outboard 100-Mbps transceivers is specified as a 40-pin cable with a 40-pin plug on one end, equipped with male jack screws that screw into mating female screw locks. The cable can be a maximum of 0.5 meters in length (about 19.6 inches). It is also possible for the outboard transceiver to be attached directly to the MII connector on the device with no intervening cable, if the design of the transceiver allows it.

Data Terminal Equipment, or Computer
The networked device itself is defined as data terminal equipment (DTE) in the IEEE standard. Each DTE attached to an Ethernet is equipped with an Ethernet interface. The Ethernet interface provides a connection to the Ethernet media system and contains the electronics and software needed to perform the medium access control functions required to send a frame over the Ethernet channel.

Note that Ethernet ports on repeaters do not use an Ethernet interface. A repeater port connects to the Fast Ethernet media system using the same PHY and MDI equipment. However, repeater ports operate at the individual bit level for Ethernet signals, moving the signals directly from segment to segment. Therefore, repeater ports do not contain Ethernet interfaces since they do not operate at the level of Ethernet frames.

On the other hand, a repeater hub may be equipped with an Ethernet interface to provide a way to communicate with the hub over the network. This allows a vendor to provide a management interface in the hub that can interact with a remote management station, using the Simple Network Management Protocol (SNMP). Managed hubs make it possible for a network manager to remotely monitor the traffic levels and error conditions on hub ports, and to shut off ports for troubleshooting, etc.

There are two kinds of repeaters in the 100BASE-T system: Class I and Class II. The standard requires that Fast Ethernet repeaters be labeled with the Roman number "I" or "II" centered within a circle. The difference between these repeaters is described in the following media chapters.

9.4 Putting it All Together

And there we have it: for a typical station connection the DTE (computer) contains an Ethernet interface which forms up and sends Ethernet frames that carry data between computers attached to the network. The Ethernet interface is attached to the media system using a set of equipment that might include an outboard MII cable and PHY (transceiver) with its associated MDI (twisted-pair RJ45-style jack or fiber optic connector). The interface or repeater port might also be designed to include the PHY electronics internally, in which case all you will see is the MDI for whatever physical medium the interface or port was designed to support. Each media type in the Fast Ethernet system has a PHY and MDI specifically designed and wired for use on that kind of segment.

CHAPTER 10 100-Mbps Twisted-Pair, Type 100BASE-TX

10.1 100-Mbps TX Media System

The 100BASE-TX interface in the figure is shown connected directly to a 100BASE-TX hub port. Outboard transceivers attached to a 40-pin MII connector on the interface or the hub could also be used to make this connection.

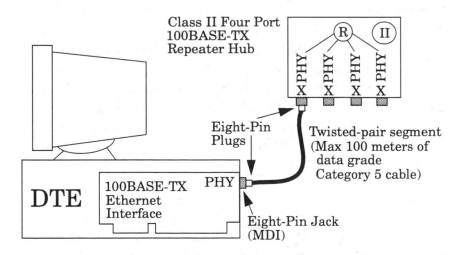

FIGURE 10.1   Connecting a computer to 100BASE-TX Ethernet

The 100BASE-TX media system is based on specifications published in the ANSI TP-PMD physical media standard. The 100BASE-TX system operates over two pairs of wires, one pair for receive data signals and the other pair for transmit data signals. Since the ANSI TP-PMD specification provides for the use of either unshielded twisted-pair or shielded twisted-pair cable, the 100BASE-TX system also does so.

The most popular wiring used today is unshielded twisted-pair cable. The two wires in each pair of the cable must be twisted together for the entire length of the segment, and kept twisted to within approximately 1/2 inch of any connector or wire termination point. This is a standard technique used to improve the signal-carrying characteristics of an unshielded wire pair.

10.2 100BASE-TX Components

The following set of components is used to build a 100BASE-TX twisted-pair segment and to make connections to it. It should be emphasized that this is just an introduction and brief survey that does not provide the detailed information you need to construct and manage media systems.

Network Medium

The 100BASE-TX media system is designed to allow segments of up to 100 meters in length when using data grade unshielded twisted-pair wire that has a characteristic impedance of 100 ohms and meets the EIA/TIA Category Five[1] wire specifications. Segments of 100BASE-TX are limited to a maximum of 100 meters to ensure that the round trip timing specifications are met. This is in contrast with the 10BASE-T media system, where the maximum segment length for the 10-Mbps link is mostly limited by signal strength.

For example, if you use high quality twisted-pair cable in a 10BASE-T segment, it's possible to reach segment lengths of approximately 150 meters with success. This is not true in the Fast Ethernet system, where the segment length for twisted-pair segments is set at a maximum of 100 meters for signal timing reasons. The EIA/TIA cabling standard recommends a segment length of 90 meters between the

---

1. The EIA/TIA wire categories are described in Appendix C.

wire termination equipment in the wiring closet, and the wall plate in the office. This provides 10 meters of cable allowance to accommodate patch cables at each end of the link, signal losses in intermediate wire terminations on the link, etc.

There are twisted-pair Ethernet cable testers available that allow you to check the electrical characteristics of the cable you use, to make sure it meets the important electrical specifications in the standard. These specifications include signal crosstalk, which is the amount of signal that crosses over between the receive and transmit pairs, and signal attenuation, which is the amount of signal loss encountered on the segment.

The 100BASE-TX media system uses two pairs of wires, which means that four pins of the eight-pin (RJ-45 style) MDI connector are used to carry Ethernet signals.

TABLE 10.1 100BASE-TX eight-pin connector

Pin Number	Signal
1	Transmit+
2	Transmit–
3	Receive+
4	Unused
5	Unused
6	Receive–
7	Unused
8	Unused

The transmit and receive data signals on each pair of a 100BASE-TX segment are polarized, with one wire of each signal pair carrying the positive (+) signal, and the other carrying the negative (–) signal.

The pin numbers used in the eight-pin connector for 100BASE-TX were changed from the ones defined in the ANSI TP-PMD standard, in order to conform to the wiring scheme already in use in the 10BASE-T standard. The ANSI standard uses pins 7 and 8 for receive data, whereas 100BASE-TX uses the same pins as the 10BASE-T system: 3 and 6. That way, a 100BASE-TX board can replace a 10BASE-T board, and be plugged into the same Category 5 wiring system without making any wiring changes.

The 100BASE-TX standard also accommodates shielded twisted-pair cabling with a characteristic impedance of 150 ohms. This type of cabling may be found in certain building cabling systems. If shielded twisted-pair cable equipped with 9-pin "D-type" connectors is used, the connector is wired according to the ANSI TP-PMD specifications: Pin 1: Receive (+), Pin 5: Transmit (+), Pin 6: Receive (−), Pin 9: Transmit (−).

100BASE-TX Repeaters

The Fast Ethernet standard defines two types of repeater: Class I and Class II. The standard requires that Fast Ethernet repeaters be labeled with the Roman number "I" or "II" centered within a circle.

A Class I repeater is allowed to have larger timing delays, and operates by translating line signals on an incoming port to digital form, and then retranslating them to line signals when sending them out on the other ports. This makes it possible to repeat signals between media segments that use different signalling techniques, such as 100BASE-TX/FX segments and 100BASE-T4 segments, allowing these segment types to be mixed within a single repeater hub. The translation process in Class I repeaters uses up a number of bit times, so that only one Class I repeater can be used in a given collision domain when maximum cable lengths are used.

A Class II repeater is restricted to smaller timing delays, and immediately repeats the incoming signal to all other ports without a translation process. To achieve the smaller timing delay, Class II repeaters connect only to segment types that use the same signalling technique, such as 100BASE-TX and 100BASE-FX segments. A maximum of two Class II repeaters can be used within a given collision domain when maximum cable lengths are used. Segment types with different signalling techniques (e.g. 100BASE-TX/FX and 100BASE-T4) typically cannot be mixed together in a Class II repeater hub.

100BASE-TX Crossover Wiring

When connecting two stations together over a segment, the transmit data pins of one MDI must be wired to the receive data pins of the other MDI, and vice versa. For a single segment connecting only two computers, you can do this by building a special crossover cable, with the transmit pins on the eight-pin plug at one end of the cable wired to the receive data pins on the eight-pin plug at the other end of the crossover cable.

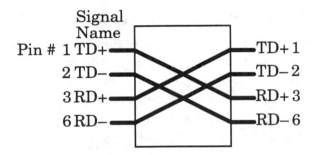

FIGURE 10.2   100BASE-TX crossover cable

However, when you are wiring multiple segments in a building, it's much easier to wire the cable connectors "straight through" and not worry about whether the wires in the jumper cables or other twisted-pair cables in your building have been correctly crossed over. The way to accomplish this is to do the crossover wiring inside the repeater hub. The 100BASE-TX standard recommends this approach, and states that each port of the hub that is crossed over internally should be marked with an "X."

100BASE-TX Link Integrity Test

The Fast Ethernet transceiver circuits (PHY) continually monitor the receive data path for activity as a means of checking that the link is working correctly. The signalling system used for 100BASE-TX segments is based on the ANSI FDDI signalling system, which sends signals continually, even during idle periods of no network traffic. Therefore, activity on the receive data path is sufficient to provide a continual check of link integrity.

Nonetheless, 100BASE-TX twisted-pair transceivers that use 8-pin MDI connectors also send and receive link pulses. These pulses are called Fast Link Pulses, and they are used in the Auto-Negotiation mechanism which allows a multi-speed hub to detect the speed of operation of an Ethernet device that is connected to it, and to adjust the speed of the hub ports accordingly. Auto-Negotiation is described in Chapter 13.

10.3 100BASE-TX Configuration Guidelines

The 100BASE-TX Ethernet segments are defined as link segments in the Ethernet specifications. A link segment is formally defined as a point-to-point medium that connects two and only two MDIs. The smallest network built with a link segment would consist of two computers, one at each end of the link segment.

TABLE 10.2 100BASE-TX segment configuration guidelines

Maximum Segment Length		Maximum Number of MAUs	
100BASE-TX	100 m (328 ft.)[a]	Per Link Segment	2

a. 100BASE-TX segments are limited to a maximum of 100 m.

A more typical installation uses multiport repeater hubs, or packet switching hubs, to provide a connection between a larger number of link segments. You connect the Ethernet interface in your computer to one end of the link segment, and the other end of the link segment is connected to the hub. That way you can attach as many link segments with their associated computers as you have hub ports, and the computers all communicate via the hub.

The 100BASE-TX specifications allow a segment of up to 100 meters. Two 100 meter 100BASE-TX segments can be connected together through a single Class I or Class II repeater. This provides a system with a total diameter of 200 meters between DTEs. The configuration rules for mixing 100 Mbps segment types and repeater types together are described in the chapter on Fast Ethernet multi-segment configuration guidelines.

10.4 100BASE-TX Twisted-Pair Physical Topology

The physical topology supported by twisted-pair link segments is the star. In this topology a set of link segments are connected to a hub, radiating out from the hub to the computers like the rays from a star. Another way to visualize the topology is as a wagon wheel, with the hub at the center and each link segment as a spoke of the wheel. This topology is shown in Figure 5.3.

CHAPTER 11   100-Mbps Fiber Optic, Type 100BASE-FX

11.1 100-Mbps Fiber Optic Media System

The 100BASE-FX interface is shown connected directly to a 100BASE-FX hub port. Outboard transceivers attached to a 40-pin MII connector on the interface or the hub could also be used to make this connection.

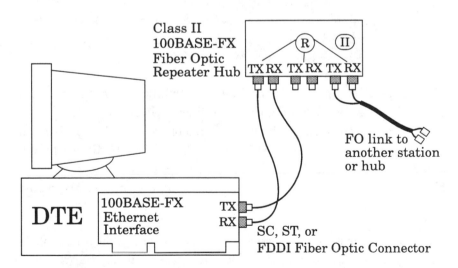

FIGURE 11.1   Connecting a computer to 100BASE-FX Ethernet

11.2 100BASE-FX Components

The following set of components is used to build a 100BASE-FX fiber optic segment, and to make connections to it. It should be emphasized that this is just an introduction and brief survey that does not provide the detailed information you need to construct and manage media systems.

Network Medium

The 100BASE-FX media system is designed to allow segments of up to 412 meters in length. While it's possible to send signals over fiber for much longer distances, the 412 meter limit for fiber segments in Fast Ethernet is there to ensure that the round trip timing specifications are met.

The 100BASE-FX specification requires two strands of multimode fiber optic (MMF) cable per link, one for transmit data, and one for receive data, with the signal crossover (TX to RX) performed in the link as shown in the figure. There are many kinds of fiber optic cables available, ranging from simple two-strand jumper cables with a PVC outer jacket material on up to large inter-building cables carrying many fibers in a bundle.

The typical fiber optic cable used for a fiber link segment is a graded index MMF cable, with a 62.5 micron fiber optic core and 125 micron outer cladding (62.5/125). The wavelength of light used on a fiber link segment is 1350 nanometers (1350 nm). There is an 11 dB loss budget allowed per link, which means that the total power loss through the fiber and associated connectors must not be higher than 11 dB as measured by a fiber optic power meter.

The more connectors you have and the longer your fiber link cable is, the higher the optical loss will be. Optical loss is measured with fiber optic test instruments that can tell you exactly how much optical loss there may be on a given segment at a given wavelength of light. A typical performance rating for standard grade fiber operating at 1350 nm will provide something in the neighborhood of from 1 dB to 2 dB loss per 1000 meters of cable. You can also expect something in the neighborhood of from 0.5 to around 2.0 dB loss per connection point, depending on how well the connection has been made. If your connectors or fiber splices are poorly made, or if there is finger oil or dust on the connector ends, then you can have higher optical loss on the segment.

MDI Connectors

The medium dependent interface (MDI) for a 100BASE-FX link may be one of three kinds of fiber optic connectors. Of the three, the duplex SC connector is the recommended alternative in the standard. The SC connector is designed for ease of use; the connector is just pushed into place and automatically completes the connection.

Another type of connector that may be used is a FDDI Media Interface Connector (MIC). This is a standard keyed connector used in the FDDI LAN system. MIC connectors are keyed in various ways, referred to as A, B, M, and S, to make sure that the FDDI cabling is connected properly. If a FDDI MIC is used as a 100BASE-FX MDI, the specifications state that it shall be keyed as an "M" receptacle. FDDI MIC connectors are also just pushed into place, and automatically complete the connection.

The third type of fiber optic connector that may be used is commonly called the ST connector. This is the same connector that is used on a 10BASE-FL link. It is a spring-loaded bayonet-type connector that has a key on an inner sleeve and also an outer bayonet ring. To make a connection, you line up the key on the inner sleeve of the ST plug with a corresponding slot on the ST receptacle, then push the connector in and lock it in place by twisting the outer bayonet ring.

100BASE-FX Repeaters

The Fast Ethernet standard defines two types of repeater: Class I and Class II. The standard requires that Fast Ethernet repeaters be labeled with the Roman number "I" or "II" centered within a circle.

A Class I repeater is allowed to have larger timing delays, and operates by translating line signals on an incoming port to digital form, and then retranslating them to line signals when sending them out on the other ports. This makes it possible to repeat signals between media segments that use different signalling techniques, such as 100BASE-TX/FX segments and 100BASE-T4 segments, allowing these segment types to be mixed within a single repeater hub. The translation process in Class I repeaters uses up a number of bit times, so that only one Class I repeater can be used in a given collision domain when maximum cable lengths are used.

A Class II repeater is restricted to smaller timing delays, and immediately repeats the incoming signal to all other ports without a translation process. To achieve the smaller timing delay, Class II repeaters connect only to segment types that use the same signalling technique, such as 100BASE-TX and 100BASE-FX segments. A maximum of two Class II repeaters can be used within a given collision domain when maximum cable lengths are used. Segment types with different signalling techniques (e.g. 100BASE-TX/FX and 100BASE-T4) typically cannot be mixed together in a Class II repeater hub.

100BASE-FX Link Integrity Test

The Fast Ethernet transceiver circuits (PHY) continually monitor the receive data path for activity as a means of checking that the link is working correctly. The signalling system used for 100BASE-FX segments is based on the ANSI FDDI signalling system, which sends signals continually, even during idle periods of no network traffic. Therefore, activity on the receive data path is sufficient to provide a continual check of link integrity.

11.3 100BASE-FX Configuration Guidelines

The 100BASE-FX Ethernet segments are defined as link segments in the Ethernet specifications. A link segment is formally defined as a point-to-point medium that connects two and only two MDIs. The smallest network built with a link segment would consist of two computers, one at each end of the link segment.

TABLE 11.1 100BASE-FX segment configuration guidelines

Maximum Segment Length		Max Number of MAUs	
100BASE-FX	412 m (1351 ft.)[a]	Per Link Segment	2

a. If a repeater is used in the link then the maximum distance allowed will be less than 412 m. Consult the multi-segment configuration rules for details.

A more typical installation uses multiport repeater hubs or packet switching hubs, to provide a connection between a larger number of link segments. You connect the Ethernet interface in your computer to one end of the link segment, and the other end of the link segment is connected to the hub. That way you can attach as many link segments with their associated computers as you have hub ports, and the computers all communicate via the hub.

Note that while a single 10BASE-FX segment may be up to 412 meters in length, when repeaters are used the maximum distance between DTEs will be less. If a single Class II repeater is used to link fiber segments, then the maximum distance between any two DTEs linked with all fiber segments may be 320 meters. This maximum distance is also called the maximum collision domain diameter. If a single Class I repeater is used, then the maximum distance between DTEs linked with all fiber segments may be 272 meters. Finally, if two Class II repeaters are used the maximum distance between two DTEs linked with all fiber segments may be 228 meters.

The configuration rules for mixing 100 Mbps segment types and repeater types together are described in the chapter on Fast Ethernet multi-segment configuration guidelines.

The physical topology supported by fiber optic link segments is the star. In this topology a set of link segments are connected to a hub, radiating out from the hub to the computers like the rays from a star. Another way to visualize the topology is as a wagon wheel, with the hub at the center and each link segment as a spoke of the wheel. This topology is shown in Figure 5.3.

CHAPTER 12 100-Mbps Twisted-Pair, Type 100BASE-T4

12.1 100-Mbps T4 Media System

The 100BASE-T4 interface is shown connected directly to a 100BASE-T4 hub port. Outboard transceivers attached to a 40-pin MII connector on the interface or the hub could also be used to make this connection.

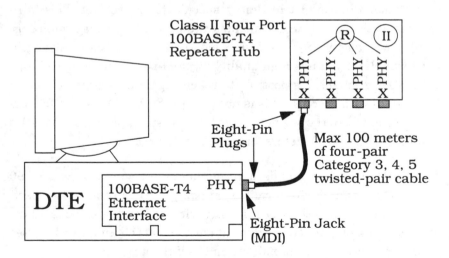

FIGURE 12.1 Connecting a computer to 100BASE-T4 Ethernet

The 100BASE-T4 system operates over four pairs of wires, with a signalling system that makes it possible to provide Fast Ethernet signals over standard voice-grade Category 3 unshielded twisted-pair cable.

12.2 100BASE-T4 Components

The following set of components is used to build a 100BASE-T4 twisted-pair segment and to make connections to it. It should be emphasized that this is just an introduction and brief survey that does not provide the detailed information you need to construct and manage media systems.

Network Medium

The 100BASE-T4 media system is designed to allow segments of up to 100 meters in length when using EIA/TIA Category 3, 4, or 5[1] unshielded twisted-pair cable. The 100BASE-T4 specifications recommend using Category 5 patch cables, jumpers and connecting hardware whenever possible, since the higher quality components and cable will improve the reception of signals on the link.

Segments of 100BASE-T4 are limited to a maximum of 100 meters, to ensure that the round trip timing specifications are met. This is in contrast with the 10BASE-T media system, where the maximum segment length for the 10-Mbps link is mostly limited by signal strength. For example, if you use high quality twisted-pair cable in a 10-Mbps 10BASE-T segment, it's possible to reach segment lengths of around 150 meters with success. This is not true in the 100-Mbps Fast Ethernet system, where the segment length for twisted-pair segments is set at a maximum of 100 meters for signal timing reasons.

The EIA/TIA cabling standard recommends a segment length of 90 meters between the wire termination equipment in the wiring closet, and the wall plate in the office. This provides 10 meters of cable allowance to accommodate patch cables at each end of the link, signal losses in intermediate wire terminations on the link, etc.

There are twisted-pair Ethernet cable testers available that allow you to check the electrical characteristics of the cable you use, to see if it

---

1. The EIA/TIA wire categories are described in Appendix C.

meets the important electrical specifications in the standard. These specifications include signal crosstalk, which is the amount of signal that crosses over between the receive and transmit pairs, and signal attenuation, which is the amount of signal loss encountered on the segment.

The 100BASE-T4 media system uses four pairs of wires, which requires that all eight pins of the eight-pin (RJ-45 style) MDI connector be used.

TABLE 12.1 100BASE-T4 eight-pin connector

Pin Number	Signal
1	TX_D1+
2	TX_D1−
3	RX_D2+
4	BI_D3+
5	BI_D3−
6	RX_D2−
7	BI_D4+
8	BI_D4−

As shown in the table, of the four pairs, one pair is for transmit data (TX), one pair is for receive data (RX), and two are bidirectional data pairs (BI). Each pair is polarized, with one wire of the pair carrying the positive (+) signal, and the other wire of the pair carrying the negative (−) signal.

100BASE-T4 Repeaters

The Fast Ethernet standard defines two types of repeater: Class I and Class II. The standard requires that Fast Ethernet repeaters be labeled with the Roman number "I" or "II" centered within a circle.

A Class I repeater is allowed to have larger timing delays, and operates by translating line signals on an incoming port to digital form, and then retranslating them to line signals when sending them out on the other ports. This makes it possible to repeat signals between media segments that use different signalling techniques, such as 100BASE-TX/FX segments and 100BASE-T4 segments, allowing these segment types to be mixed within a single repeater hub. The translation process in Class I repeaters uses up a number of bit times, so that only one Class I repeater can be used in a given collision domain when maximum cable lengths are used.

A Class II repeater is restricted to smaller timing delays, and immediately repeats the incoming signal to all other ports without a translation process. To achieve the smaller timing delay, Class II repeaters connect only to segment types that use the same signalling technique, such as 100BASE-TX and 100BASE-FX segments. A maximum of two Class II repeaters can be used within a given collision domain when maximum cable lengths are used. Segment types with different signalling techniques (e.g. 100BASE-TX/FX and 100BASE-T4) typically cannot be mixed together in a Class II repeater hub.

100BASE-T4 Crossover Wiring

A signal crossover is required between devices connected to a 100BASE-T4 segment, so that the TX data pins and bi-directional data pins on the device at one end of the segment are connected to the RX data pins and bi-directional data pins on the device at the other end, and vice versa. The standard recommends that the crossover be done internally in the repeater port. If the crossover function is done inside a repeater, then the port on the repeater must be marked with an "X."

If two stations are linked together with a single 100BASE-T4 segment, or if the repeater hub does not implement the signal crossover internally, then a special crossover cable must be provided.

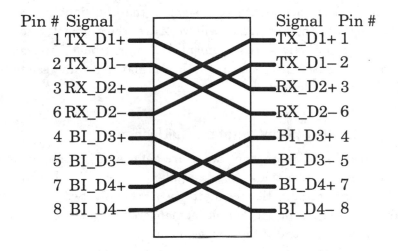

FIGURE 12.2   100BASE-T4 crossover cable wiring

As shown in the figure, a crossover cable for a 100BASE-T4 segment must be wired so that the TX pair at one end of the cable is connected to the RX pair at the other end of the cable, and vice versa. In addition, the BI_D3 pair at one end of the cable is connected to the BI_D4 pair at the other end, and vice versa.

100BASE-T4 Link Integrity Test

The Fast Ethernet transceiver circuits (PHY) continually monitor the receive data path for activity as a means of checking that the link is working correctly. When the network is idle, 100BASE-T4 transceivers send link pulses over the segment to verify link integrity. These pulses are called Fast Link Pulses, and they are also used in the Auto-Negotiation mechanism which allows a multi-speed hub to detect the speed of operation of an Ethernet device that is connected to it, and to adjust the speed of the hub ports accordingly. Auto-Negotiation is described in Chapter 13

It's important that both link lights be lit, one at each end. That indicates that there is a correctly wired signal path between both devices. However, the presence of the link lights merely means that the 100BASE-T4 segment is correctly wired. Since the link pulse operates more slowly than actual Ethernet signals, the link lights are not a guarantee that Ethernet signals will work over the segment. Odds are good that a correctly wired segment will work, but if the signal crosstalk on the segment is too high, then it may not work despite the presence of the link lights.

12.3 100BASE-T4 Configuration Guidelines

The 100BASE-T4 Ethernet segments are defined as link segments in the Ethernet specifications. A link segment is formally defined as a point-to-point medium that connects two and only two MDIs. The smallest network built with a link segment would consist of two computers, one at each end of the link segment.

TABLE 12.2 100BASE-T4 segment configuration guidelines

Maximum Segment Length		Maximum Number of MAUs	
100BASE-T4	100 m (328 ft.)[a]	Per Link Segment	2

a. 100BASE-T4 segments are limited to a maximum of 100 m.

More typical installations will use multiport repeater hubs or packet switching hubs, to provide a connection between a larger number of link segments. You connect the Ethernet interface in your computer to one end of the link segment, and the other end of the link segment is connected to the hub. That way you can attach as many link segments with their associated computers as you have hub ports, and the computers all communicate via the hub.

The 100BASE-T4 specifications allow a segment of up to 100 meters. Two 100 meter 100BASE-T4 segments can be connected together through a single Class I or Class II repeater. This provides a system with a total diameter of 200 meters between DTEs. The configuration rules for mixing 100 Mbps segment types and repeater types together are described in the chapter on Fast Ethernet multi-segment configu-ration guidelines.

12.4 100BASE-T4 Twisted-Pair Physical Topology

The physical topology supported by twisted-pair link segments is the star. In this topology a set of link segments are connected to a hub, and radiate out from the hub to the computers like the rays from a star. Another way to visualize the topology is as a wagon wheel, with the hub at the center and each link segment as a spoke of the wheel. This topology is shown in Figure 5.3.

CHAPTER 13   Auto-Negotiation

13.1 Auto-Negotiation

The Auto-Negotiation function is an optional part of the Ethernet standard that makes it possible for devices to exchange information about their abilities over a link segment. This, in turn, allows the devices to perform automatic configuration to achieve the best possible mode of operation over a link. At a minimum, Auto-Negotiation can provide automatic speed matching for multi-speed devices at each end of a link. Multi-speed Ethernet interfaces can then take advantage of the highest speed offered by a multi-speed hub port.

The Auto-Negotiation protocol includes automatic sensing for other capabilities as well. For example, a hub that is capable of supporting full duplex operation (described later in this chapter) on some or all of its ports can advertise that fact with the Auto-Negotiation protocol. Interfaces connected to the hub that also support full duplex operation can then configure themselves to use the full duplex mode in interaction with the hub.

13.2 Fast Link Pulse

Auto-Negotiation takes place using Fast Link Pulse (FLP) signals. These signals are a modified version of the Normal Link Pulse (NLP) signals used for verifying link integrity, as defined in the original 10BASE-T specifications. The FLP signals are generated automatically at power-up, or may be selected manually through the management interface to an Auto-Negotiation device.

The Fast Link Pulse signals are designed to coexist with NLP signals, so that a 10BASE-T device that uses NLP signals will continue to detect the proper link integrity even when attached to an Auto-Negotiation hub that sends FLP signals. Like the original 10BASE-T link pulse, the FLP signals take place during idle times on the network link, and do not interfere with normal traffic. Both Normal Link Pulses and Fast Link Pulses are specified only for twisted-pair media using eight-pin connectors, such as 100BASE-TX over unshielded twisted-pair. This means that network devices and repeater ports linked over fiber optic segments cannot participate in Auto Negotiation.

The FLP signals are used to send information about device capabilities. The Auto-Negotiation protocol contains rules for device configuration based on this information. This is how a hub and the device attached to that hub can automatically negotiate and configure themselves to use the highest performance mode of operation.

The Auto-Negotiation feature is optional, and therefore the Auto-Negotiation protocol is designed to work with 100BASE-T interfaces that do not support Fast Link Pulses and Auto-Negotiation, as well as older 10BASE-T interfaces. The Auto-Negotiation system also includes an optional management interface that allows you to disable Auto-Negotiation, or to manually force the negotiation process to take place. You can also use the management interface to manually select a specific operational mode for a given hub port.

13.3 Full Duplex Ethernet Links

The Auto-Negotiation protocol provides for the entire range of twisted-pair Ethernet segments, as well as full duplex Ethernet links. Full duplex Ethernet is a variant of Ethernet technology that is currently being standardized by the IEEE. In the absence of an official standard, the rules for a full duplex link length may vary depending on the vendor in question. Until the standard is complete and vendors are building equipment based on it, you cannot assume that full duplex equipment from one vendor will correctly interoperate with another vendor's equipment. Full duplex operation is briefly described here, since you may find it in use in Auto-Negotiation hubs and interfaces.

The full duplex mode of operation requires that each end of the link only connects to a single device, such as a workstation or a switched hub port. Since there are only two devices on a full duplex link, the link is not attempting to create a shared Ethernet channel capable of supporting multiple devices. Therefore, there is no need to adhere to the original Ethernet medium access control system.

With no need to use the medium access control mechanism to share the signal channel with multiple stations, a device at the end of a full duplex Ethernet link does not have to listen for other transmissions or for collisions when sending data. Full duplex operation is quite simple compared to normal Ethernet, and devices at the end of a full duplex link can send and receive data simultaneously over the link. One advantage of this approach is that the full duplex link can theoretically provide twice the bandwidth of normal (half duplex) Ethernet.

The 10BASE-T, 100BASE-TX, and 100BASE-FX signalling systems can support full duplex operation, since they have transmit and receive signal paths that can be simultaneously active. Another advantage is that full duplex fiber optic links can be much longer than the specifications for a normal 100BASE-FX segment allow. That's because the lack of any requirement to adhere to the round trip timing of a collision domain allows the fiber link to be as long as the optical loss budget permits. For that reason, a full duplex version of the 100-Mbps fiber link can typically provide a segment length of around two kilometers.

13.4 Auto-Negotiation Priorities

When two Auto-Negotiation devices with multiple capabilities are connected together, they find their highest performance mode of operation based on a priority table. The Auto-Negotiation protocol contains a set of priorities which result in the devices selecting their highest common set of abilities.

The priorities are listed in the table from the highest to the lowest. The full duplex mode of operation is given higher priority than the original (half duplex) Ethernet, since the full duplex system can send more data than a half duplex link operating at the same speed. Therefore if the devices at both ends of the link can support full duplex operation, and if they also both support Auto-Negotiation of this capability, then they will automatically configure themselves for the higher performance full duplex mode.

TABLE 13.1 Auto-Negotiation priority resolution table

A:	100BASE-TX Full Duplex
B:	100BASE-T4
C:	100BASE-TX
D:	10BASE-T Full Duplex
E:	10BASE-T

The table shows that if both devices on the link can support, for example, 10BASE-T and 100BASE-TX, then the Auto-Negotiation protocol at both ends will connect using the 100BASE-TX mode instead of 10BASE-T.

13.5 Examples of Auto-Negotiation

The following examples help to illustrate some aspects of twisted-pair link operation with and without Auto-Negotiation.

One End of Link Without Auto-Negotiation

If Auto-Negotiation only exists at one end of the link, the Auto-Negotiation protocol is designed to detect that condition and respond correctly using a mechanism called Parallel Detection. For example, if a dual-speed 10/100 Ethernet interface with Auto-Negotiation is connected to a 10BASE-T hub that does not have Auto-Negotiation, the interface will generate FLPs but will only receive NLPs from the 10BASE-T hub. The Auto-Negotiation protocol in the interface will detect the presence of Normal Link Pulses and automatically place the interface in 10BASE-T mode.

Similarly, when an Auto-Negotiation hub with multiple capabilities on its ports is connected to an interface that only supports 100BASE-TX and is not equipped with Auto-Negotiation, the Auto-Negotiation protocol will set the hub port to operate in 100BASE-TX mode. Parallel Detection works for 10BASE-T as well as 100BASE-TX and 100BASE-T4 devices without Auto-Negotiation. Parallel Detection for 100BASE-TX/T4 checks the link signals being received for Link Monitor characteristics that are specific to a given mode. If Parallel Detection determines that exactly one mode of Link Monitor is satisfied by the incoming link signals, it connects to that mode.

Operating at the Highest Performance Mode

If the 10BASE-T hub in the previous example is later replaced with a 100BASE-T repeater hub, then the dual-speed interface will receive FLPs when the hub is turned on, and the Auto-Negotiation protocol will result in the interface and hub port both operating at 100-Mbps as long as all interfaces connected to the repeater hub can operate at 100-Mbps. The switch from 10-Mbps to 100-Mbps will occur with no manual intervention.

Auto-Negotiation ensures that all devices attached to the hub are operating at the highest common denominator. Since a repeater hub is used to create a shared signal channel for all devices attached to the repeater ports, that shared signal channel must operate no faster than the slowest device attached to it.

If an Auto-Negotiation repeater hub has one of its ports attached to a device that only supports 10BASE-T, with the rest of the ports attached to 100BASE-T devices, then the hub will negotiate a speed of 10-Mbps for all ports, since that is the highest common denominator for all repeated ports. When every device attached to the repeater hub is capable of operating at 100-Mbps, then the hub will negotiate 100-Mbps for all ports.

If there is no common technology detected at either end of the link, then the Auto-Negotiation protocol will not make a connection, and the port will be left in the off condition. For example, if a 100BASE-T4 device is connected to a port on a 100BASE-TX switch, no connection will be established on that link.

Switching Hub Ports

Unlike a repeater hub, in which all ports must operate at the same speed, a switching hub provides ports that operate independently. A hub with switched ports can support 10-Mbps operation on one port, and 100-Mbps operation on another port of the same hub.

Let's consider the case of a switched port on a central hub that is attached to a link segment that connects to a repeater hub. Both hubs are equipped with Auto-Negotiation. The repeater hub, in turn, connects to several computers. In this case, the two hubs would use the Auto-Negotiation protocol on the link that connects them, and would negotiate for the highest common denominator of capabilities that can be supported on that link.

If any computer connected to the repeater hub is equipped with an interface that supports only 10BASE-T, then the repeater hub will operate all ports in 10BASE-T mode, and will also negotiate 10BASE-T operation with the switched port on the central hub. Later, when all machines on the repeater hub are capable of operating at 100BASE-TX, for example, the repeater hub will negotiate a 100BASE-TX link with the central switching hub.

Auto-Negotiation and Cable Type

The Auto-Negotiation system is designed so that a link will not become operational until matching capabilities exist at each end. However, the Auto-Negotiation protocol is not able to test the cable used on the link. Therefore, it is up to the installer to make sure that either the correct cable type is in place, or the mode of operation on the link is set correctly.

For example, consider a link with a hub at one end, a station at the other end, and with Auto-Negotiation in operation in both devices. If the cable used in this link is only rated at Category 3 then operation using 100BASE-TX on this link can be a problem. When power is applied, the hub and station will use Auto-Negotiation to determine the capabilities at each end. We will assume for the purpose of this example that the hub and station are each capable of 10BASE-T and 100BASE-TX operation and will choose to operate at the highest performance mode they have in common, which is 100BASE-TX. The Auto-Negotiation link pulses are simply bursts of the same link pulses used in 10BASE-T, so the pulses will travel over Category 3 wire without any problems and the negotiation process will work OK. However, 100BASE-TX operation requires the use of Category 5 cable, which means that this link will either operate marginally with a high rate of errors, or not at all.

While Auto-Negotiation is a handy feature that allows the highest performance mode to be automatically selected, it still requires that the correct cable type be in place for the highest speed mode that may be selected on a link. Auto-Negotiation devices also provide management capabilities that allow a network manager to set a mode for a given link, etc. By using the management interface you can make sure that a given link does not negotiate a mode of operation that exceeds the capabilities of the cabling for that link.

CHAPTER 14   100-Mbps Multi-Segment Configuration Guidelines

14.1 100-Mbps Multi-Segme nt Configuration Guidelines

This chapter describes the rules for combining multiple segments to build larger 100-Mbps Ethernets. The IEEE 802.3 standard provides two models for verifying the configuration of multi-segment 100-Mbps baseband Ethernets. The first configuration model is called Transmission System Model 1, and consists of a set of simplified configuration guidelines that can be applied to 100-Mbps Ethernet systems. The second model, Transmission System Model 2, provides a set of calculations that you can use to verify more complex 100-Mbps Ethernet topologies.

We begin by looking at the scope of the configuration guidelines, to help make it clear that the guidelines apply to a single LAN. To do that, we describe the function of a collision domain. Following that, we describe the Model 1 and Model 2 rules.

14.2 Collision Domain

The scope of the multi-segment configuration guidelines is limited to a single Ethernet, or collision domain. A collision domain is formally defined as a single CSMA/CD network in which there will be a collision if two computers attached to the system both transmit at the same time.

An Ethernet system composed of a single segment or multiple segments linked to each other with a combination of repeaters is a network that functions as a single collision domain.

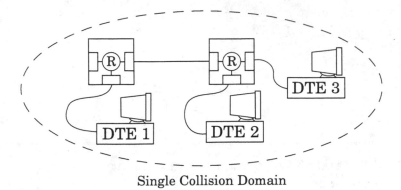

Single Collision Domain

FIGURE 14.1   Repeater hubs create a single collision domain

Figure 14.1 shows two repeater hubs connecting three computers. Since only repeater connections are used between segments in this network, all of the segments and computers are in the same collision domain.

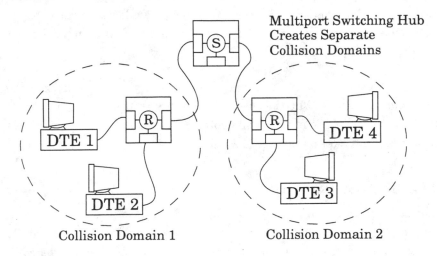

FIGURE 14.2   Switching hub creates separate collision domains

The repeaters and DTEs in Figure 14.2 are instead separated by a packet switch (switching hub, bridge, or router), and are therefore in separate collision domains, since packet switches do not forward collision signals from one segment to another. Packet switches contain multiple Ethernet interfaces, and are designed to receive a packet on one Ethernet port and transmit the data onto another Ethernet port in a new packet. Instead of propagating collision signals between Ethernet segments, packet switches interrupt the collision domain and allow the Ethernets they link to operate independently. Therefore, you can use packet switching hubs to build larger network systems by interconnecting individual Ethernet systems.

The configuration guidelines described here are from the 802.3 standard, which describes the operation of a single Ethernet LAN. Therefore, the guidelines apply to a single collision domain only and have nothing to say about combining multiple Ethernets with packet switches. As long as each collision domain is configured properly it will function correctly, and you can link many such networks together using packet switching hubs.

14.3 100-Mbps Repeater Types

The Fast Ethernet standard defines two types of repeater: Class I and Class II. The standard requires that Fast Ethernet repeaters be labeled with the Roman number "I" or "II" centered within a circle.

A Class I repeater is allowed to have larger timing delays, and operates by translating line signals on an incoming port to digital form, and then retranslating them to line signals when sending them out on the other ports. This makes it possible to repeat signals between media segments that use different signalling techniques, such as 100BASE-TX/FX segments and 100BASE-T4 segments, allowing these segment types to be mixed within a single repeater hub. The translation process in Class I repeaters uses up a number of bit times, so that only one Class I repeater can be used in a given collision domain when maximum cable lengths are used.

A Class II repeater is restricted to smaller timing delays, and immediately repeats the incoming signal to all other ports without a translation process. To achieve the smaller timing delay, Class II repeaters connect only to segment types that use the same signalling technique, such as 100BASE-TX and 100BASE-FX segments. A maximum of two Class II repeaters can be used within a given collision domain when maximum cable lengths are used. Segment types with different signalling techniques (e.g. 100BASE-TX/FX and 100BASE-T4) typically cannot be mixed together in a Class II repeater hub.

14.4 100-Mbps Configuration Guidelines: Model 1

Transmission System Model 1 of the Ethernet standard provides simplified guidelines. These make up a set of "canned" configuration rules that can be used to evaluate 100BASE-T configurations. The goal of the configuration guidelines is to make sure that the important Ethernet timing requirements are met, so that the medium access control protocol will function correctly.

1. **All copper (twisted-pair) segments must each be less than or equal to 100 meters in length.**

2. **Fiber segments must each be less than or equal to 412 meters in length.**

3. **MII cables must not exceed 0.5 meters each. When it comes to evaluating network timing, delays attributable to the MII interface do not need to be accounted for separately, since these delays are incorporated into DTE and repeater delays.[1]**

With these rules in mind, Table 14.1[2] shows the maximum collision domain diameter for segments using Class I and Class II repeaters.

---

1. Based on IEEE Std 802.3u-1995, p.29-3.
2. Based on IEEE. Std 802.3u-1995 Table 29-2, p. 29-5.

The maximum collision domain diameter is the longest distance between any two DTEs in the collision domain.

TABLE 14.1 Model 1: Maximum collision domain in meters

Repeater Type	Copper	Fiber	Copper and Fiber (T4 and FX)	Copper and Fiber (TX and FX)
DTE-DTE Single Segment	100	412	N/A	N/A
One Class I Repeater	200	272	231[a]	260.8[a]
One Class II Repeater	200	320	N/A[b]	308.8[a]
Two Class II Repeaters	205	228	N/A[b]	216.2[c]

a. Note: Assumes 100 meter copper link and one fiber link.

b. Not Applicable: T4 and FX cannot be linked with typical Class II repeater.

c. Note: Assumes 105 meters of copper link and one fiber link.

The first row in the table shows that a DTE-to-DTE (station to station) link with no intervening repeater may be made up of a maximum of 100 meters of copper, or 412 meters of fiber. The next row provides the maximum collision domain diameter when using a Class I repeater, including the case of all twisted-pair cable, all fiber optic cable, or a mix of twisted-pair and fiber. Note that in one case, a mix of T4 copper and FX fiber across a Class I repeater is shown. All other cases of mixed fiber and copper are based on TX and FX segments.

The next row shows the maximum collision domain length with a single Class II repeater in the link. The last row shows the maximum collision domain allowed when two Class II repeaters are used in the link. In this last configuration, the twisted-pair segment length is assumed to be 105 meters on the mixed fiber and twisted-pair segment. Some illustrations of example configurations may be found in Appendix B, "100-Mbps Configuration Examples."

14.5 Sample 100-Mbps Ethernet Configuration

The next figure shows one possible maximum configuration based on the 100-Mbps simplified guidelines. Note that the maximum collision domain diameter includes the distance A (100m) + B (5m) + C (100m). These segment lengths can be varied in length as long as the maximum collision domain diameter does not exceed the guidelines for the segment types and repeaters being used.

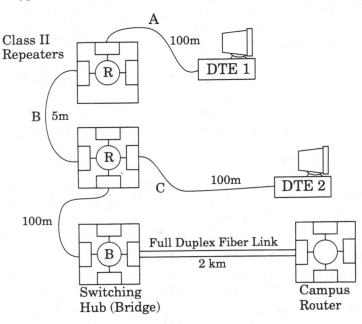

FIGURE 14.3 One possible maximum 100-Mbps configuration

In other words, the inter-repeater segment (B) in Figure 14.3 could be 10 meters in length, as long as other segment lengths are adjusted to keep the maximum collision diameter to 205 meters. You should be wary of exploiting this, however, since designing a network that relies on shorter than standard links could cause confusion and problems later on. For example, if a new segment of 100 meters is attached to the system at some later time, the maximum diameter between some DTEs could then become 210 meters. If the path delay on this long path exceeds 512 bit times, then the network may experience problems such as late collisions and CRC errors.

Note that the switching hub is just another station (DTE) as far as the guidelines for the collision domain go. The switching hub provides a way to link separate network technologies, in this case a standard 100BASE-T segment and a full-duplex Ethernet link. The switching hub is shown linked to a campus router with a full-duplex fiber link that spans up to two kilometers. This makes it possible to provide a 100-Mbps Ethernet connection to the rest of a campus network using a router port located in a central section of the campus network.

14.6 100-Mbps Configuration Guidelines: Model 2

Transmission System Model 2 for 100BASE-T segments provides a set of calculations for verifying the round trip signal delay of more complex Fast Ethernet LANs. The physical size and the number of links and repeaters in a 100BASE-T system are primarily limited by the round-trip signal timing required to ensure that the collision detect mechanism will work correctly. The Model 2 configuration calculations provide the information you need to verify the timing budget of a set of standard 100BASE-T components, to make sure that their combined signal delays fit within the timing budget required by the standard.

You may notice that these calculations appear to have a different round trip timing budget than the ones used for the 10-Mbps media system. This is because media segments in the Fast Ethernet system are based on different signalling systems than 10-Mbps Ethernet, and because the conversion of signals between the Ethernet MAC and the media segments consumes a number of bit times. You may also notice that there is no calculation for interframe gap shrinkage, unlike the 10-Mbps Model 2 rules. That's because the maximum number of repeaters allowed in a Fast Ethernet system does not result in enough gap shrinkage to worry about.

Finding the Worst-Case Path

You begin the process of checking your network by finding the path with the longest round trip time and largest number of repeaters between two stations (DTEs). In some cases you may decide that you have more than one candidate for worst-case path in your system. If that's the case, identify all the paths through your network that look like they are worst-case, then do the calculations for each worst-case path you have found. If any path exceeds the limits for round trip timing or interframe gap, then the network system does not pass the test.

Calculating Round Trip Delay Time

Once you have determined the worst-case path, you calculate the total round trip delay by taking the sum of all the individual segment delay values in the path, plus the DTE delays and repeater delays. The calculation model provides a set of delay values measured in bit times, as shown in Table 14.2.[3]

TABLE 14.2 100BASE-T component delays

Component	Delay per Meter[a]	Max Delay [b]
Two TX/FX DTEs		100
Two T4 DTEs		138
One T4 and one TX/FX DTE		127
Category 3 Cable Segment	1.14	114 (100 meters)
Category 4 Cable	1.14	114 (100 meters)
Category 5 Cable	1.112	111.2 (100 meters)
Shielded Twisted-Pair Cable	1.112	111.2 (100 meters)
Fiber Optic Cable	1.0	412 (412 meters)
Class I Repeater		140
Class II Repeater with all ports TX/FX		92
Class II Repeater with any T4 port		67

a. Round trip delay in bit times per meter.
b. Maximum round trip delay in bit times.

To calculate the round trip delay value for segments in the worst-case path, you multiply the length of the segment (in meters) times the "Delay per Meter" listed in the table for the segment type, which

3. Copyright © 1995. IEEE. Std 802.3u-1995 p. 29-8.

results in the round trip delay in bit times. If your segment is the maximum length, or if you're not sure of the segment length and want to use the maximum length in your calculations just to be safe, then instead of calculating the segment delay time you can use the "Max Delay" value listed in the table for that segment type.

Once you have calculated the segment delay values for each segment in the worst-case path on your LAN, you then add the segment delay values together, along with the delay values for two DTEs, and the delay for any repeaters in the path, to find the total path delay. Your vendor may provide values for cable, DTE, and repeater timing, which you can use instead of the ones in the table.

To this total you add a safety margin of from zero to four bit times, with four bit times of margin recommended in the standard. This helps account for unexpected delays, such as those caused by long patch cables between a wall jack in the office and the computer. **If the result is less than or equal to 512 bit times, the path passes the test**.

Segment Delay Value
The segment delay value varies depending on the kind of segment used, and on the quality of cable in the segment if it is a copper segment. More accurate cable delay values may be provided by the manufacturer of the cable used to build your segment. If you know the propagation delay of the cable you are using, you can also look up the delay for that cable in Table 14.3.

Calculating Your Own Segment Delay Values
Table 14.3 is taken from the standard and provides a set of delay values in bit times per meter, listed in terms of the speed of signal propagation on the cable. The speed (propagation time) is provided as a percentage of the speed of light (c); this is also called the "Nominal Velocity of Propagation (NVP)" in vendor literature.

If you know the propagation time (NVP) of the cable you are using, this table can provide the delay value in bit times per meter for the cable, which you can then use to find the round trip segment delay value for use in the Model 2 calculations.

TABLE 14.3 Conversion table for cable propagation times[a]

Speed Relative to C	Nanoseconds/ Meter	Bit Time/ Meter
0.4	8.34	0.834
0.5	6.67	0.667
0.51	6.54	0.654
0.52	6.41	0.641
0.53	6.29	0.629
0.54	6.18	0.618
0.55	6.06	0.606
0.56	5.96	0.596
0.57	5.85	0.585
0.58	5.75	0.575
0.5852	5.70	0.570
0.59	5.65	0.565
0.6	5.56	0.556
0.61	5.47	0.547
0.62	5.38	0.538
0.63	5.29	0.529
0.64	5.21	0.521
0.65	5.13	0.513
0.654	5.10	0.510
0.66	5.05	0.505
0.666	5.01	0.501
0.67	4.98	0.498
0.68	4.91	0.491
0.69	4.83	0.483
0.7	4.77	0.477
0.8	4.17	0.417
0.9	3.71	0.371

a. Copyright © 1995. IEEE. Std 802.3u-1995 p. 29-8, 29-9.

Typical Propagation Values for Cables

As an example of vendor NVP specifications, the next table lists some typical propagation rates provided by two major vendors of unshielded twisted-pair cables, including Category 3, 4, and 5 cables.[4]

TABLE 14.4 Typical vendor-supplied cable propagation times[a]

Vendor	Part Number	Category	Jacket	NVP
AT&T	1010	3	non-plenum	67%
AT&T	1041	4	non-plenum	70%
AT&T	1061	5	non-plenum	70%
AT&T	2010	3	plenum	70%
AT&T	2041	4	plenum	75%
AT&T	2061	5	plenum	75%
Belden	1229A	3	non-plenum	69%
Belden	1455A	4	non-plenum	72%
Belden	1583A	5	non-plenum	72%
Belden	1245A2	3	plenum	69%
Belden	1457A	4	plenum	75%
Belden	1585A	5	plenum	75%

a. For 4-pair, #24 AWG, unshielded twisted-pair cables.

14.7 Model 2 Configuration Example

Refer back to Figure 14.3, which shows one possible maximum length system. As we've seen, the Model 1 rule-based configuration method shows that this system is OK. To check that, we'll evaluate the same system using the calculation method provided in Model 2.

---

4. The EIA/TIA wire categories are described in Appendix C.

Worst-Case Path

In the example network the two longest paths are between DTE 1 and DTE 2, and between DTE 1 and the switching hub. DTE 1 must go through two repeaters and two 100 meter segments as well as a five meter inter-repeater segment to reach either DTE 2 or the switching hub. The switching hub is considered just another DTE as far as the configuration guidelines are concerned. Both of these paths in the network are the same, so we will evaluate one of them as the worst-case path. Let's assume that all three segments are 100BASE-TX segments, based on Category 5 cables. By looking up the Max Delay value in Table 14.2 for a Category 5 segment, we find 111.2 bit times.

To find the delay of the 5 meter inter-repeater segment we multiply the round trip Delay per Meter for Category 5 cable (1.112) times the length of the segment in meters (5) and end up with 1.112 x 5 = 5.56 bit times for the round trip delay. Now that we know the segment round trip delay values, we can complete the evaluation by following the steps for calculating the total round trip delay for the worst-case path.

TABLE 14.5 Round trip delay in sample network, default timing values

Two TX DTEs	100
100 m Cat 5 segment	111.2
100 m Cat 5 segment	111.2
5 m Cat 5 segment	5.56
Class II repeater[a]	92
Class II repeater[a]	92
Total Delay =	511.96

a. All ports TX/FX.

To calculate the total round-trip delay we use the delay times for DTEs and repeaters found in Table 14.2. As you can see, the total round trip path delay value for the sample network is 511.96 bit times when using Category 5 cable. This is less than the maximum of 512 bit times allowed, which means that the network passes the test for round-trip delay. Note, however, that there is no margin of up to 4 bit times provided in this calculation. The bit time values we used were all from Table 14.2, which provides worst-case values that you can use if you don't know what the actual cable values, repeater timing, or DTE timing is.

On the other hand, let's see what happens if we work this example again, using actual cable specifications provided by a vendor. Let's assume that the Category 5 cable is AT&T type 1061 cable, a non-plenum cable which has an NVP of 70% as shown in Table 14.4. If we look up that speed in Table 14.3, we find that a cable with a speed of 0.7 is rated at 0.477 bit times per meter. The round trip bit time will be twice that, or 0.954 bit times. The timing for 100 meters will therefore be 95.4 bit times, and for 5 meters it will be 4.77 bit times. Let's see how things add up using these different cable values.

TABLE 14.6 Round trip delay using vendor timing for cable

Two TX DTEs	100
100 m Cat 5 segment	95.4
100 m Cat 5 segment	95.4
5 m Cat 5 segment	4.77
Class II repeater[a]	92
Class II repeater[a]	92
Margin	4
Total Delay =	483.57

a. All ports TX/FX.

As you can see, when real-world cable values are used instead of the worst-case default values in Table 14.2 there is enough timing left to provide for 4 bit times of margin while still meeting the goal of 512 with bit times to spare.

Working With Bit Time Values

Some vendors note that their repeater delay values are smaller than the value listed in table 14.2, which will also make it easier to meet the 512 bit time maximum. While theoretically these extra bit times could be used to provide a longer than 5 meter inter-repeater segment length, for example, this approach could lead to problems.

While providing a longer inter-repeater link might seem to be an advantage, you should also consider what would happen if that vendor's repeater failed and had to be replaced with another vendor's repeater whose delay time was larger. If that happened, then the worst-case path in your network might end up with excessive delay due to the bit times consumed by the longer inter-repeater segment you had implemented. You can avoid this problem by designing your network conservatively and not pushing things to the edge of the timing budget.

Note that it is possible to use more than one Class I or two Class II repeaters in a given collision domain if the segment lengths are kept short enough to provide the extra bit time budget required by the repeaters. However, the majority of network installations are based on building cabling systems with 100 meter segment lengths (typically implemented as 90 meters "in the walls" and 10 meters for patch cables, etc.). A network design with so many repeaters that the network requires very short segments to meet the timing specifications is not going to be useful in most situations.

14.8 Network Documentation

You should document each network link in your system when it is installed. The documentation should include the length of each cable segment in the link, including any MII cables, patch cables, etc. Also included should be the cable type and any information you can collect on the cable manufacturer, cable ID numbers printed on the outer sheath, and cable delay in bit times provided by the manufacturer.

CHAPTER 15   Bridges and Switching Hubs

15.1 Linking Ethernet Segments with Bridges

So far in this guide we've described how you can build larger Ethernets by combining media segments with repeaters. Linking segments with repeaters gives you a single Ethernet (collision domain) that operates at a single bit rate of either 10-Mbps or 100-Mbps. But how do you link Ethernets that operate at different speeds? And how can you link multiple Ethernet systems at your site while controlling the flow of traffic so that not all segments are flooded with traffic? You can do this by using a bridge or switching hub to link segments instead of a repeater.

Bridges and switching hubs are more generally known as packet switches. These are devices with multiple network interfaces that operate by reading in a frame (also called a packet) on one interface, making a forwarding decision based on addresses in the frame, and potentially retransmitting the frame on another interface. When packet switches are used to link LANs they interrupt the collision domain, so that each Ethernet LAN linked with a switch operates separately. Packet switches also provide traffic control by making sure that traffic that is local to a given LAN stays on that LAN and is not sent onto the rest of the network system.

The use of packet switches to build larger network systems is a big topic, and one that cannot be fully described here. On the other hand, a form of simple packet switch known as the Ethernet bridge or switching hub is widely used to extend Ethernets, so we will describe its operation in this chapter.

Bridges and switching hubs are devices that make it possible to split up or "segment" Ethernet systems into multiple Ethernets, which makes it possible to provide more network bandwidth at your site. The most basic form of Ethernet bridge is a two-port device that allows you to link two separate Ethernet systems.

Switching hubs are multiport bridges that allow you to link a number of individual network segments or Ethernet LANs using bridging technology. Let's look next at how a bridge functions, so that you can see how a bridge makes it possible to limit the flow of traffic in an Ethernet system.

15.2 Brief Tutorial on Ethernet Bridging

A two-port bridge and a basic switching hub operate in the same way. The only difference is that a switching hub typically provides a larger set of ports designed for direct attachment to network segments. Therefore, once you know how Ethernet bridging works, you will also know how the most commonly used switching hubs work as well.

There are much more complex packet switching hubs available these days that provide such things as high-level protocol routing, but in this chapter we will only be discussing switches that do basic bridging.

Transparent Bridging

Ethernet bridges are designed so that the operation of the bridge is transparent to the stations on the network, which explains why this approach to packet switching is also called transparent bridging. This means that you can add a bridge to an Ethernet and it will automatically begin working, while the stations on the network see no change in the operation of the network.

By replacing a repeater with a bridge in a given Ethernet composed of several segments, you can create separate Ethernet LANs, which provides your network system with more bandwidth. The extra bandwidth comes from the reduced number of stations contending for access to the same LAN channel, as well as the ability of the bridge to isolate local traffic and prevent unnecessary network traffic from being sent to all segments.

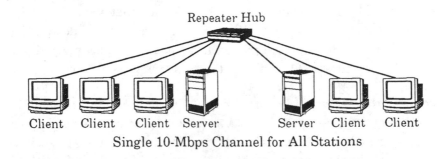

Single 10-Mbps Channel for All Stations

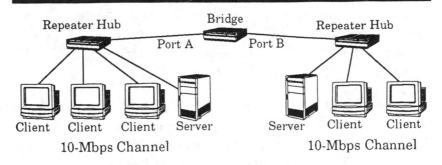

FIGURE 15.1 Bridge creates multiple Ethernet channels

A bridge controls the flow of traffic across Ethernet segments by using an automatic traffic control mechanism described in the IEEE 802.1d bridging standard. This standard describes the functions of a bridge, which includes the ability to learn station addresses and filter traffic based on the 48-bit medium access control (MAC) address.

Since traffic filtering is based on the 48-bit MAC address, you will also see this approach called "MAC layer" bridging. Another feature of the IEEE bridge standard is the ability to use something called a spanning tree algorithm to make sure that the network is kept loop free.

Address Learning

To provide automatic traffic control, bridges are designed to make traffic forwarding decisions based on the source and destination addresses of the Ethernet frames. To do this, the bridge needs a way to learn which stations are on which segments of the network.

The bridge learns the locations of stations by looking at the source addresses in all the frames it receives. Recall that when a station sends a frame it puts two addresses in the frame: the destination address of the station it is sending the frame to and a source address, which is the address of the station that is sending the frame.

The way this all works is fairly simple. Unlike a normal station that reads in only frames that are directly addressed to it, a bridge runs in what is called "promiscuous" mode, reading in all frames it sees on any of its Ethernet ports. As each frame is read in on a given port, the bridge looks at the source address of the frame and adds the source address to a database of addresses that the bridge maintains for each port. This is how the bridge figures out which stations are reachable on which ports.

This process is called adaptive filtering, and you will also see this type of bridge called a "learning bridge." Because of the ability to dynamically acquire new addresses, you can add new stations to your network without having to manually configure the bridge.

Learning bridges can also unlearn. The bridge keeps track of the age of each address entry in the address database, and deletes the entry after a period of time in which no frames are received with that source address. This allows you to move stations around from one segment to another without worrying about the bridge maintaining address tables that do not reflect current reality.

Traffic Filtering

Once the bridge has built up a database of addresses, it has the information it needs to selectively filter traffic. While the bridge is learning addresses, it is also checking each frame to make a forwarding decision based on the destination address in the frame. Let's look at how the routing decision works in a bridge equipped with two ports, Port A and Port B, as shown in Figure 15.2.

In the first example, we'll show how a bridge decides to forward a frame from one port to another. Let's assume that a frame is sent from Client 1 to Client 4. Since the frame is sent by Client 1, the bridge reads the frame in on Port A and uses its port address database to determine which of its ports is associated with the destination address in this frame.

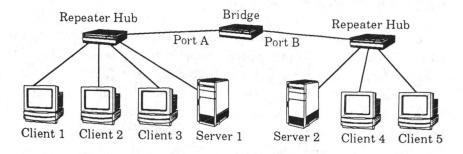

FIGURE 15.2 Traffic filtering in an Ethernet bridge

In this case the destination address of the frame corresponds to Client 4, and the bridge finds the address of Client 4 in the address database for Port B. This is how the bridge determines that this frame needs to be forwarded onto Port B in order to arrive at its destination. The bridge proceeds to transmit the frame on Port B, the frame reaches its destination, and everyone is happy.

In our next example, let's assume that the bridge receives a frame on Port A that is being sent from Client 1 to Client 2. The bridge goes through the same process of comparing the destination address of the frame (Client 2) to the list of addresses it has stored in its database of stations.

Since the destination address of the frame received on Port A matches one of the station addresses reachable on Port A, the bridge knows that the frame does not have to leave the segment to get to its destination. The bridge filters the frame by simply discarding it instead of forwarding it on to other segments. This is how a bridge isolates local traffic from the rest of the network, and prevents the flow of unnecessary traffic on a network system

If there is no match in the bridge's address database for a frame's destination address, then the bridge will forward the frame to all ports except the one it was received on, in a form of routing known as "flooding." Flooding a frame guarantees that a frame with a destination address unknown to the bridge will reach all networks linked by bridges and thereby arrive at the correct station.

Ethernet multicast frames as well as Ethernet broadcast frames are automatically flooded, so that such frames reach all stations. This is an important point: by default the bridge does not filter multicasts and broadcasts, since it is designed to make all Ethernets linked together operate transparently as though they were one large Ethernet. Therefore, a bridge behaves like a repeater for multicast and broadcast packets, and sends them out all ports.

A problem with the station learning and frame forwarding mechanism is that it's possible for parallel bridges to get into a forwarding loop, generating excess frames until the traffic rate gets so high that the network is saturated. This is unfortunate, since in a sufficiently complex network system it can be difficult to know whether or not the bridges are capable of forming loop paths. To prevent forwarding loops, the IEEE 802.1d bridging standard provides a spanning tree algorithm. Let's look at how the spanning tree algorithm works next.

Spanning Tree Algorithm

The purpose of the spanning tree algorithm is to allow the bridges in a given Ethernet system to dynamically create a loop-free set of paths. An Ethernet system must never have a loop path in it. The spanning tree algorithm makes sure that this is the case even in a complex system with lots of paths through bridges and switching hubs.

The operation of the spanning tree algorithm is based on configuration messages sent by each bridge, using a multicast address that has been reserved for bridge management. All bridges are programmed to listen for frames sent to this address, so that every bridge can send and receive configuration messages.

The configuration messages contain the information that allows a set of bridges to automatically elect a "root" bridge. The election is based on the value of Ethernet addresses in each bridge, among other items. All other things being equal, the bridge with the lowest numerical value Ethernet address is elected the root bridge. The root bridge then proceeds to send out configuration messages. Each bridge uses the information in the configuration messages it receives to calculate the best path from itself to the root bridge.

The configuration information is designed to make it possible for each bridge to select the ports that will be included in the spanning tree, and to automatically shut off those ports that could cause a loop path to occur. This ability to shut off ports is the mechanism that insures that a set of bridges can automatically configure themselves to produce loop-free paths in a complex network system.

The original spanning tree protocol was developed at Digital Equipment Corporation. It has since been superseded by the spanning tree protocol described in the IEEE 802.1d bridge standard. The IEEE spanning tree system is the one currently used by all Ethernet vendors, so that you can buy Ethernet bridges and switching hubs from a range of vendors and they will all work together to produce a set of loop-free paths in your network.

15.3 Using Switches to Improve Network Operation

Ethernet bridging technology was first delivered in the mid-1980s in the form of two-port devices that could help split a large Ethernet into separate Ethernet LANs. As the cost of the bridge electronics dropped and the performance of bridging chips improved, it became possible to build multiport bridges, generally known as switching hubs.

A basic switching hub performs the same traffic filtering and spanning tree functions as the original two-port bridge. There are a wide range of switching hubs available today, and some of the newer hubs have sophisticated added features including the routing of high-level protocols and provision for the support of multiple LAN technologies.

So far we've seen the mechanisms used by Ethernet bridges and switching hubs to automatically filter traffic and produce loop free paths in a complex system. We've also seen that a bridge or switching hub makes it possible to build a larger network by linking multiple Ethernets. Next we'll look at how switching hubs can improve the operation of a given network design.

Improved Performance Based on Traffic Control

The primary way in which any bridge or switching hub improves the operation of a network system is by controlling the flow of traffic. The ability to control traffic makes the bridge a useful tool for the Ethernet designer faced with growing station populations and increased traffic loads.

With careful design of network segments and location of the bridges, you can keep local traffic limited to a smaller set of network segments. Unlike a design based on repeaters, where all links in the network see all the traffic in the system, a design based on bridges or switching hubs will limit the traffic seen by individual links. This allows the total network system at your site to grow larger without compromising the traffic handling ability of individual links.

Switching hubs can help isolate local traffic generated by a cluster of high performance servers and client workstations from the larger network system.

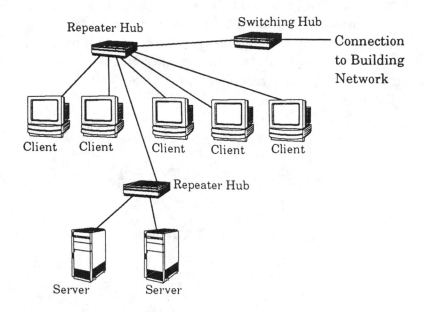

FIGURE 15.3   Isolating client-server traffic from building network

For example, Figure 15.3 shows a set of clients and two servers with a switching hub isolating their traffic from the rest of the network segments in the building. In this configuration, all of the local traffic between the clients and the servers stays local and is not sent over the rest of the building network, due to the traffic filtering capabilities of the bridge.

When using switching hubs you need to think carefully about the flow of traffic in your system. When installing a switching hub, you want to do what you can to make sure that the traffic which is local to a cluster of servers and clients stays local. In Figure 15.3 we accomplished this by locating the hub at the edge of the server-client cluster, where the connection to the rest of the building network is made.

Improved Performance By Linking Different Speed LANs

Another major advantage of a switching hub is that it can link LAN segments that operate at different speeds. This is possible since a switching hub can read in a frame on a port operating at 10-Mbps, store the frame in local memory, and then send the frame out on a port that operates at 100-Mbps. This cannot be done with repeaters, since all segments linked with a given repeater hub must operate at the same speed. The next figure shows a multi-speed switching hub being used to provide high speed access to a server.

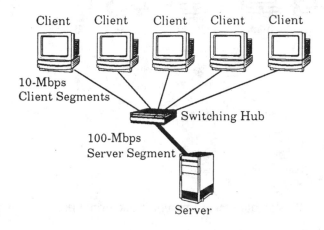

FIGURE 15.4   Switching hub linking multiple speed segments

In this network design, the server is connected to a 100-Mbps Fast Ethernet segment that is attached to the multi-speed switching hub. The client machines each connect to 10-Mbps switching ports on the hub. Since every port on the hub is a switched port, each client gets its own 10-Mbps Ethernet channel into the hub. Access to the server is by way of the 100-Mbps link, which helps make sure that the client traffic cannot overwhelm the server segment.

This last point is important and deserves to be emphasized. In this network design, it's likely that the clients will all be trying to retrieve data from the server, and the connection to the server could be overwhelmed. If the server port only operated at 10-Mbps and all clients sent a frame to the server at the same instant, the switch would have to store the frames in a temporary buffer memory while sending them out onto the server segment.

If there is a high traffic rate coming in from multiple ports, all destined for a single port, then it's possible to overrun the ability of the switching hub to temporarily store frames, in which case the switch will drop the frames. This causes the client to retransmit the data, and could lead to a slow response for the application that is losing frames while trying to talk to the server. Linking the server to the switching hub with a Fast Ethernet segment that moves data ten times faster than the client segments helps make sure that the server segment is not a bottleneck.

Hybrid Switching and Repeating Hubs

Vendors are now providing hybrid hubs that include both repeating and switching functions, and that include support for multi-speed LAN segments as well.

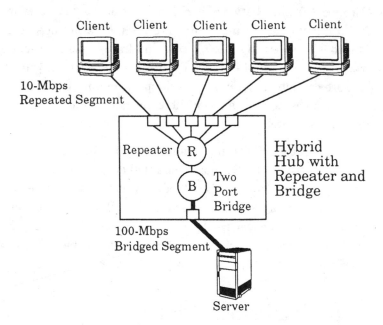

FIGURE 15.5   Hybrid switching and repeating hub

As an example of this approach, this hub contains both a five-port repeater and a two-port bridge. One port of the bridge operates at 10-Mbps, and the other port operates at 100-Mbps. This hub allows you to link five clients with a single 10-Mbps Ethernet channel by way of the repeater. The repeater is then linked to one port of the bridging switch inside the hub. The 100-Mbps port of the switch provides an external port for a high speed connection to the server.

15.4 Performance Issues

It's up to you to make sure that the switch you buy has enough performance to do the job. If you are buying a switch for use in an existing network you may want to borrow one from the vendor for a few days and try it out first, to make sure that it can handle the traffic loads on your network. We'll look next at some performance issues that are involved in evaluating a switch.

A single Ethernet LAN (collision domain) is a machine designed to move Ethernet frames between computers. It operates at a known bit rate and a known maximum frame rate.[1] All Ethernet segments of a given speed will have the same bit rate and frame rate characteristics. However, when you add a switch to your network system, you are creating a more complex machine. Now the performance of your LAN is a combination of the performance of the Ethernet segments and the performance of the switch.

Switches are equipped with multiple Ethernet interfaces. Each interface can send bits over the Ethernet channel at the speed of the Ethernet media system to which it is attached. But the performance of the switch itself may not be able to sustain the full frame rate coming in from all ports. In other words, should all ports simultaneously present high traffic loads to the switch, the switch may not be able to handle the full traffic rate and will begin dropping frames.

---

1. For example, a 10-Mbps network can send 14,880 frames per second using the minimum frame size of 64 bytes.

Typical switch hardware has special support circuits that are designed to help improve the speed with which the switch can handle a frame and look up frame addresses in the address filtering database. The special circuits and high speed buffer memory are more expensive components. The total performance of a switch is a trade-off between the cost of high speed memory and other high performance components, and the price most customers are willing to pay.

Therefore, you will find that not all switches perform alike. Some less expensive devices may have lower packet forwarding performance, smaller filtering tables, smaller buffers, etc. Larger switches with more ports will typically have higher performance and a higher price tag as well. Switches that are capable of handling the maximum frame rate on their ports are sometimes described as operating at "full wire speed" or "full media speed."

No matter how fast the switch is, it may still drop frames if a given port gets too busy and runs out of resources. These days, many high-performance workstations can send frames for sustained periods of time at the maximum frame rate. If a set of high performance clients on multiple ports of a switch simultaneously send frames to a single server port, it's possible to overrun the buffers on that port, which results in lost frames.

A dropped frame is dealt with by network protocols at the higher layers of network operation. These protocols keep track of the protocol packets being sent in the frames and detect missing packets, resending packets as required. While these protocols are designed to automatically recover from such occurrences, if there are enough dropped frames you could see a major reduction in throughput as the network application keeps having to detect and resend lost frames.

Switch performance is typically rated in terms of packets per second that the bridge can filter and forward. This gives you a rough idea of how good the performance of the bridge may be in your system. However, the rates of filtering and forwarding are only two measures of switch performance.

Since switches contain store and forward packet logic, there is also a small storage memory, known as the packet queue, for frames as they are read in. A larger packet queue allows a bridge to handle longer streams of back-to-back frames. This gives the bridge improved performance in the presence of bursts of traffic on the LAN that are generated by some file sharing network applications, for example.

As you can see, the subject of packet switch performance can get complex rather quickly. When using switches you need to keep your traffic requirements in mind. If your network includes high performance clients, all making requests from a single server or set of servers, then you may wish to investigate high performance switches. You should also pay careful attention to the placement and configuration of switches in your network system, to avoid setting up traffic bottlenecks.

10-Mbps Configuration
Examples

A.1 Summary of 10-Mbps Configuration Rules

The appendix provides a quick look at several configuration examples.
We begin by listing the configuration rules for the 10-Mbps segments.

TABLE 1.1 Summary of 10-Mbps segment configuration rules

Maximum Segment Length		Maximum Number of MAUs[a]	
10BASE5 thick coax	500 m (1640 ft.)	Per 10BASE5 Seg.	100
10BASE2 thin coax	185 m (606.9 ft.)	Per 10BASE2 Seg.	30
FOIRL fiber optic	1.0 km (3280 ft.)	Per FOIRL Segment	2
10BASE-FL fiber optic	2.0 km (6561 ft.)[b]	Per 10BASE-FL Seg.	2
10BASE-T twisted-pair	100 m (328 ft.)[c]	Per 10BASE-T Seg.	2
AUI	50 m (164 ft.)		

a. The maximum number of stations that may be in a collision domain is
1024. This limit is set by the collision backoff algorithm.

b. If 10BASE-FL MAUs are used at each end of the segment, then the segment may be up to 2000m. If one end of the segment uses an FOIRL
MAU, then the segment may only be a maximum of 1000m.

c. 10BASE-T segments may be longer while still meeting electrical specifications, depending on the quality of the twisted-pair segment.

A.2 Sample 10-Mbps Configurations

In this appendix we provide a look at several Ethernet configurations.
These configurations are not provided as examples of the "best" possi-

ble design. It's impossible to provide a single design or even set of designs that is optimal for all network situations. Instead, these configuration examples are simply provided as further illustrations of how things can be connected together.

We'll start with an Ethernet topology used in the earliest systems, which is based on a coaxial cable backbone.

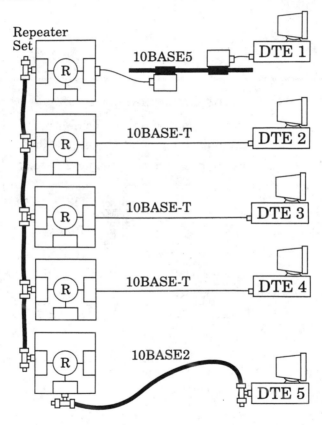

FIGURE A.1   Five repeaters in series on coax backbone

Figure A.1 shows five repeaters connected to a common backbone segment, and connecting in turn over various segment types to five DTEs. This is one way to configure a system with more than four repeaters. A typical network design based on this configuration would locate the repeaters in the same equipment closet, linking them together with short 10BASE2 cables.

Note that even though there are a total of five repeaters in this design, the fact that they are connected together over a single coaxial backbone segment means that there are no more than two repeaters in the signal path between any two DTEs, which meets the configuration guidelines.

Limits to Coaxial Designs

There are significant limits to the configuration shown in Figure A.1. For one thing, the 10BASE2 segment that links all repeaters only operates at 10-Mbps, which limits the speed of your network system. Since much of the cost of installing a network system is in the labor and time required to install the cabling, many sites prefer to install and use media segments that can handle higher speeds, which allows an upgrade path to Fast Ethernet.

Another limit to this design is that any failure on the single coaxial backbone segment will disrupt communication between the repeater hubs. If one of the 10BASE2 backbone cable segments comes loose or is removed for any reason, the entire coaxial segment will stop working, making it impossible for any of the repeaters to send data to one another over the backbone cable.

Stackable Repeaters Reduce Repeater Hop Count

If you want to provide media segments that will be capable of running at higher speeds you must use a star topology with point-to-point link segments, since Fast Ethernet segments are based on twisted-pair and fiber optic link segments. An advantage of this approach is that there are only two devices on a given link segment; this limits the effect that any segment failure may have on your total network system.

In the next figure we show five separate repeater devices. In this case, the repeaters are stackable repeaters, and the top two repeaters are shown linked together over an expansion bus. This assumes that the top two repeaters are located close to one another, since the expansion bus for stackable repeaters is typically only a half meter (1.6 feet) or so in length. Connecting the stackable repeaters together with the expansion bus makes the ports in those separate repeater boxes function as though the ports were on a single device. As a result, DTE1 and DTE2 are effectively connected to the same repeater.

All other repeaters in this configuration are linked together with point-to-point link segments. As a result of this design, there are a total of four repeater hops between DTE1 and DTE5. If the top two repeaters had not been stackable, there would have been five repeaters in the longest path between two DTEs in this network.

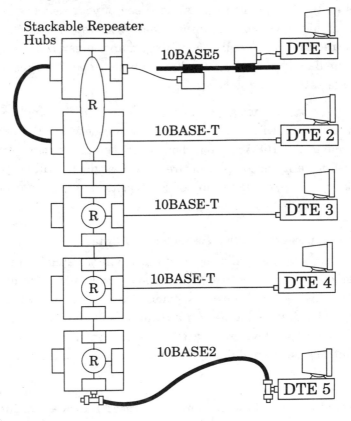

FIGURE A.2   Stackable repeaters reduce repeater hop count

This design does not provide any expansion capability for future network growth, since it is at the maximum number of repeater hops. A more desirable design would reduce the number of repeaters used, perhaps by reconfiguring the system as shown in the next design.

Fiber Optic Repeater Hub

A widely used design based on a fiber optic repeater hub is shown next. The fiber optic hub is used to provide a set of connections to other hubs in a building. In this design, the fiber optic hub becomes the backbone system for the network.

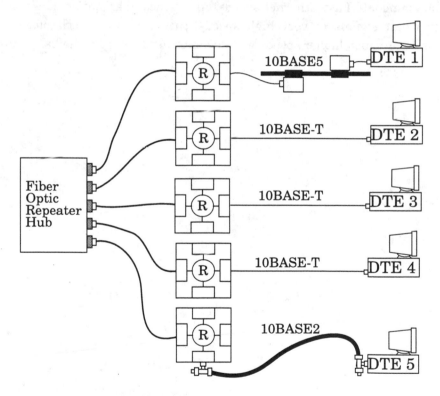

FIGURE A.3   Fiber optic backbone hub

The fiber optic hub may link to a single hub on each floor, or several hubs on a floor may be linked together and a link segment from the stack of hubs connected back to the fiber optic hub. This is another way that stackable hubs can come in handy to hold down the total number of repeater hops in a collision domain. As your network system grows you can also upgrade your hubs as required. For example, some repeater hubs might be replaced with switching hubs, to provide increased bandwidth by segmenting the network into several independent Ethernets. Adding switching hubs should be done carefully, however, to make sure that the traffic in your network does not encounter bottlenecks.

The use of fiber optic media for your backbone segments provides greater flexibility for future upgrades. Fiber optic segments can easily accommodate Fast Ethernet speeds. Also, since fiber optic media can transmit signals at very high speeds, future network technologies based on much higher speeds will no doubt use fiber optic media.

APPENDIX B   100-Mbps Configuration Examples

B.1 Summary of 100-Mbps Configuration Rules

This Appendix provides a quick look at several 100-Mbps configuration examples. We begin by listing the configuration rules for the 100-Mbps segments.

TABLE 2.1 Summary of 100-Mbps segment configuration rules[a]

Maximum Segment Length		Max. Number of Attachments	
100BASE-TX	100 m (328 ft.)[b]	100BASE-TX Segment	2
100BASE-FX	412 m (1351 ft.)[c]	100BASE-FX Segment	2
100BASE-T4	100 m (328 ft.)[d]	100BASE-T4 Segment	2
MII	0.5 m (1.6 ft.)[e]		

a. The maximum number of stations that may be in a single collision domain is 1024. This limit is set by the collision backoff algorithm.

b. 100BASE-TX segments are limited to a maximum of 100 m each.

c. A single 100BASE-FX segment may be a maximum of 412 m. If a repeater is used to link two 100BASE-FX segments, then the maximum distance between stations linked by fiber will be less than 412 m. See the multi-segment configuration guidelines for details.

d. 100BASE-T4 segments are limited to a maximum of 100 m each.

e. Maximum of two MIIs per segment, provides a maximum of 1 m of MII cable per segment.

B.2 Sample 100-Mbps Configurations

In this appendix we provide several Fast Ethernet configuration examples. We begin with a couple of simple configurations, and then show a more complex configuration using a switching hub.

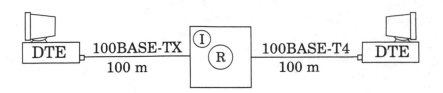

FIGURE B.1   100BASE-TX and 100BASE-T4 segments linked with Class I repeater

A Class I repeater allows you to connect segment types with different signalling systems to the same repeater hub. For example, both the TX and FX segment types use the same signalling system, which is based on the ANSI FDDI standard. The T4 system uses a different signalling system to provide Ethernet signals over four pairs of Category 3 cable. Class I repeaters make it possible to link T4 segments with TX or FX segments. The maximum collision domain diameter (maximum distance from DTE to DTE) in a system using a Class I repeater and twisted-pair cables is 200 meters.

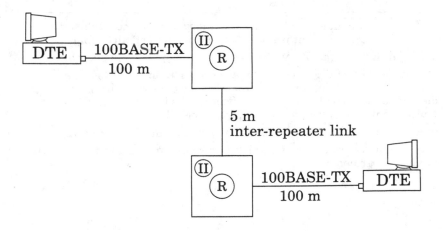

FIGURE B.2   Class II repeaters with inter-repeater link

Figure B.2 shows two Class II repeaters linking two DTEs with 100BASE-TX segments, which use Category 5 cable. The maximum diameter of a system with two Class II repeaters and twisted-pair segments is 205 meters. If both DTE segments are 100 meters, that leaves five meters for the inter-repeater link. If the DTE segments are shorter, then the inter-repeater link may be longer, provided that the maximum DTE-to-DTE diameter of the system does not exceed 205 meters.

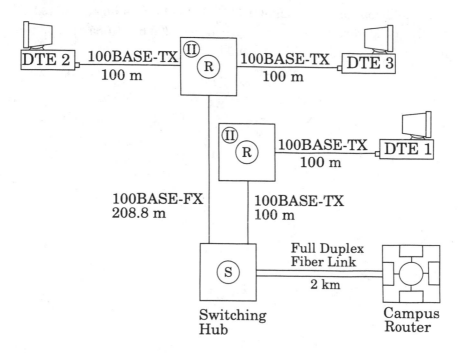

FIGURE B.3   A more complex Fast Ethernet configuration

Figure B.3 shows a more complex configuration. In this example, a switching hub in the building is providing a connection between a campus router and the network segments in the building. Since both the campus router and the switching hub are stations (DTEs), a full duplex fiber link can be used to connect the two, with a maximum distance of 2 km (6562 ft.).

A switching hub has a network interface on each switched port, and is treated as a station (DTE) as far as the configuration guidelines are concerned. In the path between the switching hub and DTE 1 there are two 100BASE-TX segments, linked with a Class II repeater. In the path between the switching hub and either DTE 2 or DTE 3, there is a 100BASE-FX fiber optic segment and a 100BASE-TX segment. Since there is only one Class II repeater in the path between the switching hub and the other DTEs, the configuration guidelines allow a maximum collision domain diameter of 308.8 meters. Subtracting 100 m for the twisted-pair segment length leaves 208.8 m (685 ft.) for the fiber optic link in this collision domain.

APPENDIX C   EIA/TIA Twisted-Pair Cable Specifications

C.1 EIA/TIA Cable Categories

Twisted-pair cable for use in Ethernet systems is typically rated in terms of which "category" of cable specifications it meets. The category system of cable specifications was first published in 1991, as part of the EIA/TIA 568-1991 Commercial Building Telecommunications Wiring Standard. The category specifications from this standard are widely used in the network industry to identify which types of twisted-pair cable can accommodate 10-Mbps and 100-Mbps data signals.

The Electronic Industries Association (EIA) and the Telecommunications Industry Association (TIA) jointly developed and published the EIA/TIA-568 commercial building wiring standard. The standard describes a uniform wiring system designed to support multiproduct, multivendor environments, including typical designs that can accommodate the communications equipment you are likely to find in an office building.

The standard also includes descriptions of the elements in a basic wiring system structure, including horizontal (single floor) and backbone (building riser) components, as well as specifying what kind of wire to use in each. You will also find references in the 568 standard to other EIA/TIA standards that describe specifications for components of the wiring system such as telecommunications closets, equipment rooms, and so on.

Finally, the 568 standard lists several cabling choices that you may wish to provide in a building, including the twisted-pair system needed to support twisted-pair Ethernet segments. Along with the 568 standard, the EIA/TIA have published several additions to the standard in the form of bulletins, one of which describes the "categories" for twisted-pair wire.

These categories provide exact information as to what kinds of electrical signals a given type of twisted-pair cable is capable of transmitting. What follows is a brief description of the EIA/TIA categories. Quotations are from an EIA/TIA technical bulletin.

- Category 1 and 2: "These cables are not covered by this bulletin and are not recognized in the ANSI/EIA/TIA 568-1991 standard. They are typically used for voice and low speed data transmission." These two categories are for older wire that was originally used for telephone systems and that is not recommended for 10BASE-T Ethernet.
- Category 3: "This designation applies to cables currently specified in the ANSI/ EIA.TIA 568-1991 standard. The characteristics of these cables are specified up to 16 MHz." Twisted-pair cables that meet the specifications for this category are rated for 10BASE-T Ethernet.
- Category 4: "The characteristics of these cables are specified up to 20 MHz." Since Category 4 cables have better signal handling characteristics than Category 3, they meet the specifications for carrying 10BASE-T Ethernet signals.
- Category 5: "The characteristics of these cables are specified up to 100 MHz." These include cables that are rated for use in anything from 10BASE-T Ethernet on up to 100BASE-T Fast Ethernet segments.

Note that the official Category system only includes specifications for Categories 3, 4, and 5. Category 1 and 2 cables are excluded since they are not recommended for data applications.

C.2 Category 5 Cables and Segment Components

Twisted-pair cable rated to meet the Category 5 cable specifications is the most widely used cable in new network installations. The reason for this is simple; for a slightly higher cost than using Category 3 cable, Category 5 cable provides you with a twisted-pair cabling system that can handle both 10-Mbps and 100-Mbps Ethernet signals.

One thing to be aware of, however, is that the cable is just one component of a typical twisted-pair segment. The entire segment (link) will typically include a jumper cable (patch cable) from the Ethernet hub in the wiring closet to a wire termination panel of some sort. From the wire termination point, which might be a "punch down" block or set of eight-pin (RJ-45 style) connectors in a patch panel, the segment then travels through the walls and over ceilings until it reaches the office. In the office the segment cable will typically be terminated in a wall plate. The wall plate is equipped with an eight-pin jack, and to make a connection to a workstation in the office you need to connect another jumper from the wall plate to the eight-pin jack in the computer. The portion of the segment between the wall plate in the office and the wire termination point in the wiring closet should be limited to 90 meters, which allows 10 meters for patch cables.

As you can see, there are a number of components in the total link that makes up the signal path of a typical twisted-pair network segment. To make sure that the entire segment can carry 100-Mbps signals without excessive signal distortion, crosstalk, or signal loss, all the components must be correctly installed and should be rated to meet Category 5 specifications. For example, a standard telephone type voice-grade RJ-45 connector does not meet the Category 5 specifications. You must make sure to get eight-pin "RJ-45 style" connectors that are specifically designed to be Category 5 connectors.

C.3 Component Specifications

As part of the 568 standards effort, there have been a series of technical service bulletins (TSB) developed that describe additional specifications for unshielded (UTP) and shielded (STP) twisted-pair connecting hardware. These include TSB 40-A-1994, "Additional Specifications for UTP Connecting Hardware," and TSB 53-1992, "Additional Specifications for STP Connecting Hardware."

Technical standards undergo fairly constant revision and updating, and the 568 standard is no exception. A new version of 568 has been developed and is known as TIA/EIA 568A. (The order of the TIA/EIA initials has been changed in the new version.) This new version includes all the relevant areas of the original 568 standard and the technical bulletins.

Link Performance Specification

As we've seen, the total link includes more than just the twisted-pair cable. However, the Category specifications only describe specific components, such as the cable or the connectors. In the real world, network administrators need to verify the performance of complete links, which include the total set of cable and connectors and wire termination points that make up the complete network segment.

The 568A standard includes new link performance specifications, and a companion technical bulletin includes new link testing specifications that describe field test procedures and include recommendations for making useful measurements of link performance. These specifications help improve the ability to make reliable tests of total link performance. Given the number of components that can be used in a segment, this turns out to be a difficult engineering issue.

C.4 Testing Twisted-Pair Segments

A quick way to "test" a twisted-pair segment is to connect Ethernet equipment to each end and see if the link lights come on. If the link lights are lit at both ends of the segment, then the odds are pretty good that the segment will function correctly. This is especially true for 10BASE-T segments, since the 10BASE-T system is designed to operate over Category 3 (modern "voice-grade" telephone cable), as well as Category 4 or 5 cable.

Increasing the speed to 100-Mbps also increases the engineering challenge of carrying high speed signals over twisted-pair cabling. That's why you must use Category 5 cable and components for 100BASE-TX segments. And that's why the standard recommends using Category 5 components, such as eight-pin connectors and patch panels, on 100BASE-T4 links as well.

To make sure that the links in your network meet the specifications you can test the links with any of a number of wire test instruments on the market today. These testers come in a range of prices and capabilities. At the least you need a test instrument that will check the important electrical characteristics of a link, to see if they meet the Category 3, 4, or 5 cable specifications as well as the Ethernet segment specifications. At a minimum a wire tester should check for:

• Continuity. This is a check to make sure that the link is wired correctly, and that the wires are continuous from end to end.

• Attenuation. This refers to the amount of signal loss over the link at the signal frequency of interest. For example, the 10BASE-T specifications allow for a maximum signal loss of 11.5 decibels (dB) for the entire link at the signal frequency used by 10-Mbps Ethernet.

• Crosstalk. Crosstalk occurs when a signal in one pair of wires is electromagnetically coupled (crosses over) to an adjacent pair; it appears as noise interference.

There are many other tests that can be performed, and it's up to you to find a wire tester that meets your needs and budget.

List of Resources

The following is a list of resources that may be consulted for further information. Several items listed here are provided with Internet addresses in the form of the Uniform Resource Locators (URLs) used by World Wide Web browsers.

Ethernet World Wide Web Site

A wide range of Ethernet resources may be found on this World Wide Web site at URL:

http://www.ots.utexas.edu/ethernet/ethernet.html

The Ethernet Web site includes on-line versions of the configuration guidelines, a list of network vendors, technical papers on Ethernet, pointers to other Web pages with Ethernet information, etc.

IEEE and DIX Standards

The formal standards are a moving target, since new standards are continually being created and old standards are continually updated. Starting as a multi-vendor standard from DEC, Intel, and Xerox (DIX), the Ethernet system became a national standard (IEEE/ANSI), and the IEEE specifications are also published as an international standard (ISO/IEC). New varieties of Ethernet media systems are developed as IEEE standards, which then become part of future editions of the International Organization for Standardization (ISO) document.

This information is taken from the 1995 IEEE Standards Catalog. This catalog may be accessed on the Internet via World Wide Web at URL:

http://stdsbbs.ieee.org:70/0/pub/ieeestds.htm

Copies of the IEEE standards may be ordered from the IEEE catalog by calling 1.800.678.IEEE in the US and Canada, or 908.981.1393 outside of the US and Canada. The address is:

IEEE Customer Service
445 Hoes Lane
PO Box 1331
Piscataway NJ 08855-1331 USA

ISO/IEC 8802-3 Document

The latest international standard for Ethernet has the following title.

- 8802-3: 1993 [ANSI/IEEE Std 802.3, 1993 Edition] Information technology—Local and metropolitan area networks—Part 3: Carrier sense multiple access with collision detection (CSMA/CD) access method and physical layer specifications

  This document includes ANSI/IEEE Std 802.3b-1985, ANSI/IEEE Std 802.3c-1985, ANSI/IEEE Std 802.3d-1987, ANSI/IEEE Std 802.3h-1990, ANSI/IEEE Std 802.3i-1990 Price US $114.00, Order # SH16337

The 802.3j-1993 supplement which describes the 10-Mbps fiber optic media system, and the 802.3u supplement, which describes the entire 100-Mbps Fast Ethernet system, have not made it into the ISO 8802-3 document as yet. The 802.3j supplement is available for US $70.00, and a final draft version of the 802.3u supplement is available for US $67.00.

DIX Ethernet Standard

A Ethernet equipment since 1985 is built according to the IEEE standard. However, the original DIX Ethernet specification is still available, and may be purchased from Digital. The title of the document is:

- Version 2.0, DEC-Intel-Xerox (DIX) Ethernet Standard, Ethernet Local Area Network Specification Version 2.0. November, 1982 Price: US $30.00, Order Number: AA-K759B-TK Order from: DEC Direct: 1.800.344.4825

IEEE 802.12 — 100VG-AnyLAN

The IEEE 802.12 standard describes another approach to transmitting Ethernet frames at 100-Mbps that uses a different medium access control mechanism. A copy of the 802.12 standard can be acquired from the IEEE.

Networking Periodicals

There are a number of magazines and trade journals that cover networking issues and that provide a guide to the networking marketplace. A few of the more LAN-oriented ones are listed here. Most of the trade journals are not for sale. Instead, you can request a free qualification form, and if you are employed in the field or otherwise involved in networking you may qualify for a free subscription.

- Cabling Business Magazine
Monthly magazine, available free to qualified subscribers
12035 Shiloh Rd. Suite 350
Dallas, TX 75228-9601
214.328.1717

- Communications Week, The Newspaper For Network Decision Makers
Weekly tabloid, available to qualified subscribers
Communications Week
PO Box 2070
Manhasset, NY 11030
URL: **http://techweb.cmp.com/techweb/cw**

- Data Communications, McGraw Hill's Networking Technology Magazine
Monthly magazine, available free to qualified subscribers or may be purchased
Data Communications
McGraw-Hill Building
1221 Avenue of the Americas
New York, N.Y. 10020
Subscription services: 800.525.5003, or 609.426.7070

- InfoWorld
Weekly tabloid, available free to qualified subscribers
Infoworld Publishing Co.

155 Bovet Road Suite 800
San Mateo, CA 94402
415.572.7341
URL: **http://www.infoworld.com**

• LAN, The Local Area Network Magazine
Miller Freeman Publications
Subscription Services
PO Box 41904
Nashville, TN 37204
800.933.3321, or 615.377.3322
URL: **http://www.lanmag.com**

• LAN Times
Monthly magazine, available free to qualified subscribers
1900 O'Farrell St. 2nd Floor
San Mateo, CA 94403
URL: **http://www.wcmh.com/lantimes**

• Network Computing
Monthly magazine, available free to qualified subscribers
Network Computing
2800 Campus Drive
San Mateo, CA 94403
Subscription services: 708.647.6834
URL: **http://techweb.cmp.com/nwc**

TIA/EIA 568A Cabling Standard

The TIA/EIA cabling standards provide guidelines for installing, terminating, and testing twisted-pair cabling systems. The specifications for cable categories and other practices described in these standards are widely adopted in the networking industry. The latest version of the TIA/EIA 568A Commercial Building Telecommunications Cabling standard is available from Global Engineering Documents. Global sells copies of all the TIA/EIA standards documents, including the various technical service bulletins.

Global Engineering Documents
15 Inverness Way East
Englewood, CO 80112
800.854.7179
303.792.2181

Glossary

ANSI: ANSI American National Standards Institute. The coordinating body for voluntary standards groups within the United States. ANSI is a member of the International Organization for Standardization (ISO).

ARP: Address Resolution Protocol. A protocol used to discover a destination host's hardware (MAC) address when given the host's IP address.

Attenuation: The decreasing power of a transmitted signal as it travels along a cable. The longer a cable the more attenuation there will be. After a certain amount of attenuation, the cable may not transmit data reliably.

AUI: Attachment Unit Interface. The IEEE 802.3 name for the cable connecting the MAU to the networked device. In the original DIX standard the MAU is called a transceiver, and the AUI is called a transceiver cable. The AUI cable is equipped with 15-pin connectors, and the mating 15-pin connector on a network device is commonly referred to as the AUI connector.

Backbone: The part of the network that is used as a primary path for transporting traffic between network segments.

BNC: A bayonet locking connector used on 10BASE2 thin coaxial cable segments. The BNC designation is said to be short for Bayonet Navy Connector, however it is also said to stand for Bayonet Neil-Concelman after the names of two designers of coaxial connectors.

Category 3, Category 5: A Telecommunications Industry Association/Electronics Industry Association (TIA/EIA) standard that specifies commercial building telecommunications cable according to a set of categories. Category 3 cable has electrical characteristics suitable for carrying 10BASE-T and 100BASE-T4 signals. Category 5 cable has higher performance characteristics needed to carry 100BASE-TX signals.

Coaxial Cable: A type of cable known for low susceptibility to interference. An outer conductor, also called a screen or shield, surrounds an inner conductor. The conductors are commonly separated by a solid plastic or foam plastic insulating material.

Collision: A normal event on Ethernet that indicates simultaneous channel access by two or more stations. A collision is automatically resolved by the medium access control mechanism.

Crossover Cable: A patch cable wired in such a way as to route the transmit signals from one piece of equipment to the receive signals of another piece of equipment, and vice versa.

Crosstalk: The unwanted transfer of a signal from one circuit, called the disturbing circuit, to another, called the disturbed circuit. In twisted-pair cables, the unwanted transfer of signals from transmitting wires to other wires in the cable plant.

CSMA/CD: Carrier Sense Multiple Access/Collision Detect. The formal name for the medium access control mechanism used in Ethernet.

DTE: Data Terminal Equipment. The data station (computer) or port serving as the data source, destination, or both, for the purpose of sending or receiving data on a network.

Eight-Pin Connector: A twisted-pair connector that resembles the RJ-45 connector used in US telephone systems. The IEEE 802.3 standard recommends that eight-pin connectors used in 100BASE-T systems have a Category 5 rating.

Fast Link Pulse: A link pulse which encodes information used in the Auto-Negotiation protocol on 100BASE-T twisted-pair links. Fast link pulses consist of bursts of the normal link pulses used in 10BASE-T.

FDDI: Fiber Distributed Data Interface. An ANSI standard (ANSI X3T9.5) for a 100-Mbps token passing network based on fiber-optic and twisted-pair cable.

Fiber Optic Cable: Glass filament cable which transmits digital signals in the form of light pulses.

Fifty-Pin Connector: Commonly referred to as a Telco connector, this connector is used on 10BASE-T hubs as an alternate twisted-pair segment connection method. The 50-pin connector connects to 25-pair cables, which are frequently used in telephone wiring systems and which typically meet Category 3 specifications.

Late Collision: A failure of the network in which the collision indication arrives too late in the frame transmission to be automatically dealt with by the medium access control mechanism. The frame being transmitted will be dropped due to data errors, which requires that the application detect the loss and retransmit the frame. This can result in greatly reduced throughput. Late collisions may be caused by an overlong media system with excessive round trip timing delay, or by excessive levels of signal crosstalk in a twisted-pair cabling system.

Link Light: Optional status light on a MAU that indicates the status of the link integrity test. If this light is lit on the MAUs at both ends of the link, it indicates that the link has passed the link integrity test.

Link Pulse: A test pulse sent between MAUs on the link segment during periods of no traffic, to test the signal integrity of the link.

Link Segment: Defined in the IEEE 802.3 specifications as a point-to-point segment that connects two and only two MDIs.

MAU: Medium Attachment Unit. The IEEE 802.3 name for the device used in 10-Mbps Ethernet systems to transmit and receive signals between the Ethernet interface and the media segment. This device is called a transceiver in the original DIX Ethernet standard.

MDI: Medium Dependent Interface. The name for the connection method used to make a physical and electrical connection between a MAU and a media segment. The eight-pin RJ-45 style connector is the MDI for the 10BASE-T, 100BASE-TX and 100BASE-T4 media systems.

MIC: Media Interface Connector. Specified for use in the FDDI LAN system to make a connection to a pair of fiber optic cables. May also be used in the 100BASE-FX media system. However, the SC connector is listed in the specifications as the preferred connector for 100BASE-FX.

MII: Medium Independent Interface. In the 100-Mbps Fast Ethernet system this optional interface provides a 40-pin connection to outboard transceivers (called PHY devices) that can connect to a 10BASE-T segment or any of the 100BASE-T media types.

Mixing Segment: Defined in the IEEE 802.3 specifications as a segment that may have more than two MDI connections.

N Connector: A coaxial cable connector used for 10BASE-5 thick coax segments.

Patch Cable: A twisted-pair or fiber optic jumper cable used to make a connection between a network interface on a station or network port on a hub and a media segment.

Phantom Collision: In twisted-pair Ethernet systems a phantom collision can be caused by excessive crosstalk. Collisions are detected on twisted-pair segments by the simultaneous presence of signal on the transmit and receive signal pairs. Excessive crosstalk can appear as a false, or phantom, collision indication to the transmitting interface.

PHY: Physical Layer Device. In Fast Ethernet this is an outboard transceiver that is attached to the 40-pin MII connector.

Receive Collision: A collision detected by a device that is not actively transmitting. When a receive collision is detected by an Ethernet repeater, it will transmit a collision enforcement jam signal on all other ports.

RJ-45: See eight-pin connector.

SC: A type of fiber optic connector used in the 100BASE-FX Fast Ethernet fiber optic media system. The connector is designed to be pushed into place, and automatically seats itself.

Silver Satin: Name for the silver-grey voice grade patch cable used to connect a telephone to a wall jack. Typical silver satin patch cables do not have twisted pair wires, which makes them unsuitable for use in an Ethernet system. The lack of twisted-pairs will result in high levels of crosstalk, which can lead to slow performance on the link.

SQE: Signal Quality Error. This signal indicates the detection of a collision on the medium by the MAU. The original DIX Ethernet standard referred to this signal as Collision Presence. In the IEEE 802.3 specifications the name was changed to SQE.

SQE Test: This signal tests the SQE detection and signalling circuits. The original DIX Ethernet standard referred to this signal as Collision Presence Test, also known as "heartbeat." The name was changed to SQE Test in the IEEE 802.3 specifications.

ST: A type of fiber optic connector used in 10BASE-FL and FOIRL links. The male end of this connector has an inner sleeve with a slot cut into it, and an outer ring with a bayonet latch. The inner sleeve is aligned with a mating key in the socket, and the outer ring is turned to complete the bayonet latch.

Telco Connector: See Fifty-Pin Connector.

Terminator: For copper cable a terminator prevents signal reflections by acting like a sponge a soaking the signals up when they reach the end of the cable instead of letting them bounce back and interfere with other signals. Thick and thin coaxial Ethernet require 50-ohm terminators that are connected to each end of the coaxial segment. There must be exactly two terminators on every coaxial segment.

Transceiver: See MAU.

Twisted-Pair: A multiple-conductor cable whose component cables are paired together, twisted, and enclosed in a single jacket. A typical Category 5 twisted-pair segment is composed of a cable with four twisted pairs contained in a single jacket. Each pair consists of two insulated copper wires twisted together. The twists are varied in length to reduce the potential for signal interference between pairs.

Voice Grade: A term for twisted-pair cable used in telephone systems to carry voice signals. Category 3 voice grade cable can carry 10BASE-T and 100BASE-T4 signals.

Index